CAMBRIDGE PRIMARY
Mathematics

Skills Builder

5

Name: _____

Contents

Mary Wood

CAMBRIDGE
UNIVERSITY PRESS

CAMBRIDGE
UNIVERSITY PRESS

University Printing House, Cambridge CB2 8BS, United Kingdom

Cambridge University Press is part of the University of Cambridge.

It furthers the University's mission by disseminating knowledge in the pursuit of education, learning and research at the highest international levels of excellence.

www.cambridge.org
Information on this title: education.cambridge.org/9781316509173

© Cambridge University Press 2016

First published 2016

Printed Poland by Opolgraf

A catalogue record for this publication is available from the British Library

ISBN 978-1-316-50917-3 Paperback

This book is part of the Cambridge Primary Maths project. This is an innovative combination of curriculum and resources designed to support teachers and learners to succeed in primary mathematics through best-practice international maths teaching and a problem-solving approach.

To get involved, visit
www.cie.org.uk/cambridgeprimarymaths.

Introduction

This *Skills Builder activity book* is part of a series of 12 write-in activity books for primary mathematics grades 1–6. It can be used as a standalone book, but the content also complements *Cambridge Primary Maths*. Learners progress at different rates, so this series provides a Skills Builder and a Challenge Activity Book for each Primary Mathematics Curriculum Framework Stage to support and broaden the depth of learning.

The *Skills Builder* books consolidate the learning already covered in the classroom, but provide extra support by giving short reminders of key information, topic vocabulary and hints on how best to develop maths skills and knowledge. They have also been written to support learners whose first language is not English.

How to use the books

The activities are for use by learners in school or at home, ideally with adult support. Topics have been carefully chosen to focus on those common areas where learners might need extra support. The approach is linked directly to *Cambridge Primary Maths*, but teachers and parents can pick and choose which activities to cover, or go through the books in sequence.

The varied set of activities grow in challenge through each unit, including:

- closed questions with answers, so progress can be checked
- questions with more than one possible answer
- activities requiring resources, for example, dice, spinners or digit cards
- activities and games best done with someone else, for example, in class or at home, which give the opportunity to be fully involved in the child's learning
- activities to support different learning styles: working individually, in pairs, in groups.

How to approach the activities

Space is provided for learners to write their answers in the book. Some activities might need further practice or writing, so students could be given a blank notebook at the start of the year to use alongside the book. Each activity follows a standard structure.

- **Remember** gives an overview of key learning points. They introduce core concepts and, later, can be used as a revision guide. These sections should be read with an adult who can check that the learner understands the material before attempting the activities.
- **Vocabulary** assists with difficult mathematical terms, particularly when English is not the learner's first language. Learners should read through the key vocabulary. Where necessary, they should be encouraged to clarify their understanding by using a mathematical dictionary or, ideally, by seeking adult help.

- **Hints** prompt and assist in building understanding, and steer the learner in the right direction.
- **You will need** gives learners, teachers and parents a list of resources for each activity.
- **Photocopiable resources** are provided at the end of the book, for easy assembly in class or at home.
- **Links** to the Cambridge International Examinations Primary Mathematics Curriculum Framework objectives and the corresponding *Cambridge Primary Mathematics Teacher's Resource* are given in the footnote on every page.
- **Calculators** should be used to help learners understand numbers and the number system, including place value and properties of numbers. From Stage 5, learners are expected to become proficient in using calculators in appropriate situations. This book develops the learner's knowledge of number without a calculator, although calculators can be useful for checking work.

Note:

When a 'spinner' is included, put a paperclip flat on the page so the end is over the centre of the spinner. Place the pencil point in the centre of the spinner, through the paperclip. Hold the pencil firmly and spin the paperclip to generate a result.

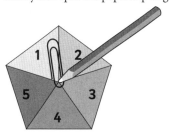

Tracking progress

Answers to closed questions are given at the back of the book; these allow teachers, parents and learners to check their work.

When completing each activity, teachers and parents are advised to encourage self-assessment by asking the students how straightforward they found the activity. When learners are reflecting on games, they should consider how challenging the mathematics was, not who won. Learners could use a ✓/ ✗ or red/green colouring system to record their self-assessment for each activity.

These assessments provide teachers and parents with an understanding of how best to support individual learners' next steps.

Place value

Remember

Place value – the ten digits 0, 1, 2, 3, 4, 5, 6, 7, 8 and 9 are used to build up large numbers.

- When you multiply numbers by 10 or 100 all the digits move 1 or 2 places to the left.
- When you divide numbers by 10 or 100 all the digits move 1 or 2 places to the right.

Example:
$356\ 900 \div 100 = 3569$
$3569 \times 10 = 356\ 900$

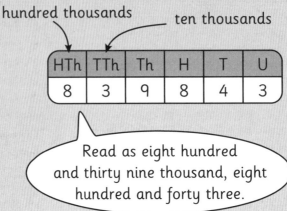

hundred thousands   ten thousands

HTh	TTh	Th	H	T	U
8	3	9	8	4	3

Read as eight hundred and thirty nine thousand, eight hundred and forty three.

---

1 What is the value of the digit 9 in the number 498 316? Circle the correct answer.

      nine million   nine hundred   nine thousand

      ninety thousand   nine hundred thousand

Hint: Use a place-value chart to help you.

2 Here are some number cards.

    1 **9** **3** **5** **7**

You can use each card once, to make a number like this.

    9 **1** **3** **5** **7**

(a) What is the biggest number you can make with the five cards? _____

(b) What is the smallest number you can make with the five cards? _____

(c) Write your answers in words.

_____

_____

3 Identify the operations missing from the loops

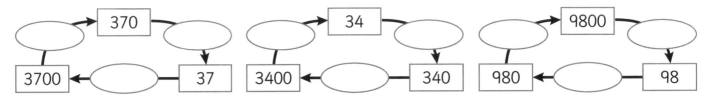

4 Place value challenge – a game for two players

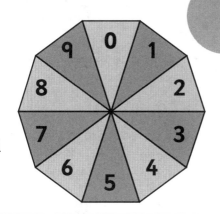

Use the spinner and a game board.

Take turns to spin the spinner and write your number in any cell on the game board. The winner is the player with the highest number when all the boxes have been filled.

Game 1	HTh	TTh	Th	H	T	U
Player 1						
Player 2						

Game 2	HTh	TTh	Th	H	T	U
Player 1						
Player 2						

Hint: Think carefully before placing each number. Remember, you can use any cell. Practise saying the numbers.

5 Complete the table for each function machine.

IN → ×10 → OUT

IN	3489		45 678		18 700	
OUT		8640		379 020		18 700

If you know the 'out' number you need to divide by 10 to find the 'in' number, for example:

$8640 \div 10 = 864$

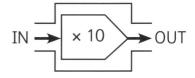

IN → ÷100 → OUT

IN	54 800		45 100		18 700	
OUT		8640		9020		1870

If you know the 'out' number you need to multiply by 100 to find the 'in' number, for example:

$8640 \times 100 = 864 000$

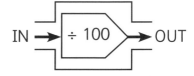

Ordering and rounding

Remember

When comparing numbers:

< means 'is less than' for example 515 005 < 515 505

> means 'is greater than', for example 515 505 > 515 005

When rounding numbers:

to the nearest 10 look at the units digit so 2364 rounds down to 2360

to the nearest 100 look at the tens digit so 2364 rounds up to 2400

to the nearest 1000 look at the hundreds digit so 2364 rounds down to 2000

1 Write the correct sign, < or >, between the numbers in each pair.

4567 ☐ 4657   5454 ☐ 5054   34 686 ☐ 35 860

7878 ☐ 7808   65 646 ☐ 65 628   654 659 ☐ 654 751

> **Hint:** The point of the symbol always points to the smaller number.
>
> small < large   large > small

2 Use the digits 2, 3, 5 and 7 to make five different four-digit numbers.
Use 2, 3, 5 and 7 in each of your numbers.

☐☐☐☐ ☐☐☐☐ ☐☐☐☐ ☐☐☐☐ ☐☐☐☐

Write the numbers in order starting with the smallest.

_____ _____ _____ _____ _____

3 Use the spinner twenty five times.
Write the numbers in the boxes to give five five-digit numbers.

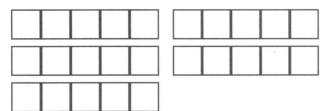
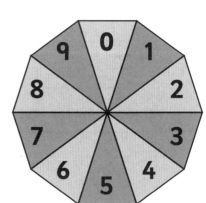

Write the numbers in order starting with the smallest.

_____ _____ _____

Unit 1A: Number and problem solving
CPM framework 5Nn6, 5Nn8; Teacher's Resource 1.2

4 Complete this table to show numbers rounded to the nearest 100.

	rounded to the nearest 100
456	
4562	
45 628	
456 281	

Hint: Using a number line can help you.

Use this line to help you with the next part of the table.

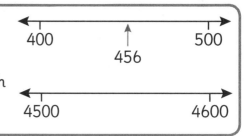

5 Which number in the list satisfies all the clues? _____

3826   3778   3783   3762   3781   3819   3772   3779

- the number is 3800 to the nearest 100
- the number is 3780 to the nearest 10
- the number is even.

Hint: You can use the clues in any order. Try crossing out the numbers that do not satisfy the clue. You should have just one number left.

Write the eight numbers in order starting with the smallest number.

_____

6 Rounding up or down – a game for two players

Use the spinner and the record sheet below.

Player 1 spins the spinner four times to create a four-digit number.
Player 2 rounds the number to the nearest 100.

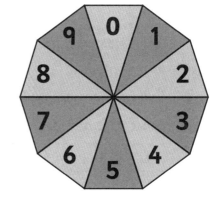

Example:

1st spin	2nd spin	3rd spin	4th spin
3	8	6	5

3865 rounds up to 3900

Hint:

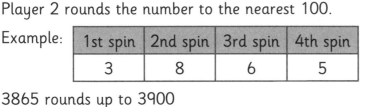

If the number rounds up the player scores 1 point and if the number rounds down they score 2 points. In the example, 3865 rounds up so only scores 1 point.

Swap roles and repeat. After five turns each the winner is the player with the higher score.

Player 1		Player 2	
Number	Score	Number	Score
Total		Total	

Sequences and general statements

Remember

To work out the pattern in a **sequence**, look at the difference between each consecutive number. Each of these numbers is referred to as a **term**.

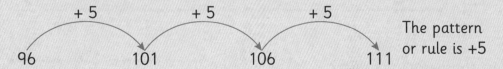

The pattern or rule is +5

A **general statement** is a rule that always works.
You might be asked to find examples that match a general statement or find a counter-example to show that a statement is false.

Example 1: Find three examples to match the statement, 'the sum of three odd numbers is odd.'
1 + 3 + 5 = 9, 3 + 3 + 3 = 9 and 13 + 7 + 23 = 43

Example 2: Alma says, 'When you halve an even number the answer is always an odd number.' Is Alma correct? Explain how you know.
4 ÷ 2 = 2 and 2 is even so Alma is not correct.

You will need:
sets of digit cards from resource 1, page 80, for activity 5

Vocabulary
pattern, sequence, rule, term, general statement

---

1 Follow the rules to shade in the numbers.

Start at 2 and count in threes.

1	2	3	4	5
6	7	8	9	10
11	12	13	14	15
16	17	18	19	20
21	22	23	24	25

Start at 1 and count in threes.

1	2	3	4	5
6	7	8	9	10
11	12	13	14	15
16	17	18	19	20
21	22	23	24	25

Start at 3 and count in fours.

1	2	3	4	5	6
7	8	9	10	11	12
13	14	15	16	17	18
19	20	21	22	23	24
25	26	27	28	29	30
31	32	33	34	35	36

2 A sequence starts 1, 4, 7, 10, 13 ....

What is the rule for the sequence?

Hint: Can you spot this sequence in the diagrams for activity 1? Look to see which grid it is in.

Unit 1A: Number and problem solving, Unit 2A: Number and problem solving
CPM framework 5Nn1, 5Nn12, 5Nn13, 5Nn14, 5Ps6, 5Ps8; Teacher's Resource 1.3, 10.1 Sequences, 10.2

3 Noura makes a sequence of numbers, starting with 10. She subtracts 4 each time.
What are the next three numbers in the sequence?

_____ _____ _____

Hint: It may be helpful to draw a number line.

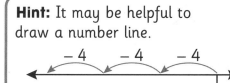

4 This is part of a number sequence.

| 150 | 155 | 160 | 165 | 170 |

The sequence continues.

Hint: Diagrams like this show that the sequence continues in both directions.

Circle **all** the numbers that would appear in the sequence.

120   230   30   189   1000   153

5 Odds and evens – a game for two players

Each player needs a set of 1–9 digit cards, shuffled and placed face down. Both players turn over the top card from their pile. If the sum is even player 1 gets a point, if the sum is odd player 2 gets a point.

Hint: To find the sum, add the two numbers together, for example the sum of 4 and 3 is 4 + 3 = 7

The first player to gain 10 points wins the game.

Record your results in the first three columns of the table:

Sum	Score		Result
	Player 1	Player 2	
Example: 5 + 7 = 12	1		odd + odd = even

Hint: The statements in the results columns are general statements.

Complete the final column using only odd, even, +, =.

6 Find three examples that match each of these general statements.

- The sum of two even numbers is even. _____

- The sum of three odd numbers is odd. _____

Unit 1A: Number and problem solving, Unit 2A: Number and problem solving
CPM framework 5Nn1, 5Nn12, 5Nn13, 5Nn14, 5Ps6, 5Ps8; Teacher's Resource 1.3, 10.1 Sequences, 10.2

9

Addition and subtraction

Remember

Addition

Use any method for addition that you feel you can use quickly and efficiently.

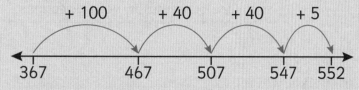

```
367
+185
400   300 + 100
140   60 + 80
 12   7 + 5
552
```

```
367
+185
 12
145
400
552
```

```
367
+185
552
 1 1
```

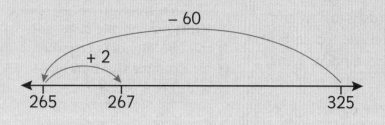

Subtraction

Subtract: 325 – 58

Use whichever method you prefer, to work quickly and efficiently.

```
200 +110 +15
 –      50   8
200 + 60 + 7
```

```
²3²¹¹2¹5
–   58
267
```

1 Highest score – a game for two players

Take turns to spin the spinner and write down the number in one of the boxes in your grid.

Continue until all the boxes are filled.

Add the two three-digit numbers.

The player with the higher total wins.
The first player to win three rounds is the champion.

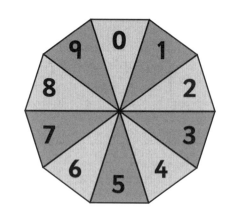

Player 1

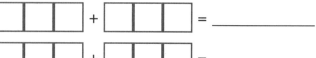

Player 2

Explain to the other player how you work out each answer.

Record the calculation and the method.

Unit 1A: Number and problem solving, **Unit 2A:** Number and problem solving, **Unit 3A:** Number and problem solving
CPM framework 5Nc18, 5Nc19, 5Ps2; Teacher's Resource 2.1, 2.2, 13.1, 13.2, 25.1

2   Lowest score – a game for two players

Take turns to spin the spinner and write down the number in one of the boxes in your grid, below.

Continue until all the boxes are filled.

Complete the subtraction.

Record the calculation and the method.

Explain to the other player how you work out your answer.

The player with the lower answer wins.
The first player to win three rounds is the champion.

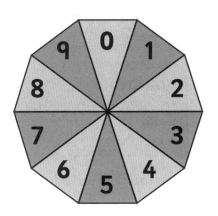

Player 1   **Player 2**

☐☐☐ – ☐☐☐ = _____   ☐☐☐ – ☐☐☐ = _____

☐☐☐ – ☐☐☐ = _____   ☐☐☐ – ☐☐☐ = _____

☐☐☐ – ☐☐☐ = _____   ☐☐☐ – ☐☐☐ = _____

☐☐☐ – ☐☐☐ = _____   ☐☐☐ – ☐☐☐ = _____

☐☐☐ – ☐☐☐ = _____   ☐☐☐ – ☐☐☐ = _____

3   Use whichever method you prefer to work these out.

$346 - 155 =$

$924 - 405 =$

Unit 1A: Number and problem solving, Unit 2A: Number and problem solving, Unit 3A: Number and problem solving
CPM framework 5Nc18, 5Nc19, 5Ps2; Teacher's Resource 2.1, 2.2, 13.1, 13.2, 25.1

Multiplication by a single digit

Remember

Here are three methods for multiplying a two-digit number by a single digit.

Example 126 × 5

Method 1: Partitioning

126 × 5 = (100 × 5) + (20 × 5) + (6 × 5)

         = 500 + 100 + 30

         = 630

Method 2: Grid method

×	100	20	6
5	500	100	30

500 + 100 + 30 = 630

Method 3: Compact method

```
100 + 20 + 6                    126
      × 5                       × 5
  ─────────                     ─────
   500  100 × 5    ──→           500
   100   20 × 5                  100
    30    6 × 5                   30
  ─────                         ─────
   630                           630
```

All these methods work but a compact method is quick to use, provided you understand it.

Vocabulary

digit, partition, grid method, multiplication, product

---

1 Look at this multiplication grid.

×	30	6
7	210	42

210 + 42 = 252

36 × 7 = 252

3.6 × 7 = 25.2

Work out these pairs of calculations.

(a) 38 × 3   (b) 49 × 5

     3.8 × 3   4.9 × 5

Hint: You can use any method you like to multiply.

36 × 7 = 252

3.6 is 10 times smaller than 36 so the answer to 3.6 × 7 is ten times smaller than 252.

3.6 × 7 = 25.2

Unit 1A: Number and problem solving
CPM framework 5Nc20, 5Nc22, 5Ps2; Teacher's Resource 3.2

2 Dice multiplication – a game for two players

Use the spinner and the recording grids below.

Player 1 spins the spinner three times to make a three-digit number. They write it on the record sheet then spin the spinner again and record the single digit number. Player 2 does the same.

Both players multiply their two numbers together and write the answers in the answer box. The winner of the round is the player with the larger answer. The overall winner is the player who wins more rounds.

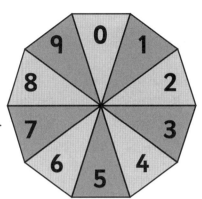

Example round:

	Player 1	Player 2
3-digit number	639	742
1-digit number	4	3
Answer	2556	2226

Winner
Player 1

Hint: Use this game as a way of practiscing multiplication. Discuss the methods you use with your partner and check each other's answers.

	Player 1	Player 2
3-digit number		
1-digit number		
Answer		

Winner

Working out

	Player 1	Player 2
3-digit number		
1-digit number		
Answer		

Winner

Working out

	Player 1	Player 2
3-digit number		
1-digit number		
Answer		

Winner

Working out

	Player 1	Player 2
3-digit number		
1-digit number		
Answer		

Winner

Working out

Written methods of multiplication

Remember

When multiplying a two-digit number by a two-digit number you can use the grid method.

Example 46 × 13

×	40	6
10	400	60
3	120	18

400 + 120 + 60 + 18 = 598

You will need: counters

Vocabulary
grid method, partition, multiplication, product

Choose the product – a game for two players

You will need some counters or you could cross through the numbers instead.

Players take turns to choose one number from Group A and one number from Group B then find the product of the two numbers. If the answer corresponds with a number on the large grid the player places a counter on the number. The winner is the first player to have four counters in a row horizontally, vertically or diagonally.

> **Hint:** Use this game as a way of practising multiplication. Discuss the methods you use with your partner and check each other's answers.

Group A   75   56   25   27   19

Group B   15   37   8   24   49

456	1566	375	1225	931
1450	285	2072	703	4350
999	1800	1102	840	1323
2744	600	1344	2775	405
3248	648	3675	1125	925

Unit 1A: Number and problem solving
CPM framework 5Nc21; Teacher's Resource 3.3

Show your working here.

Division

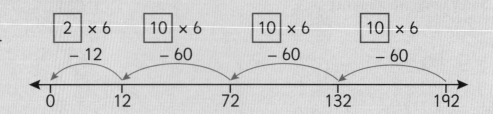

Remember

1 You can use a number line to divide.

$192 \div 6 = 32$

2 Division is repeated subtraction.

```
    192
 –   60    10 × 6
    132
 –   60    10 × 6
     72
 –   60    10 × 6
     12
 –   12    2 × 6
      0    32 × 6
```

3 Compact repeated subtraction

```
    192
 –  180    30 × 6
     12
 –   12    2 × 6
      0    32 × 6
```

You can use any of these methods. The third method (compact repeated subtraction) is the shortest and most efficient but only use it if you are confident.

---

1 Use a number line to complete these division calculations.

Vocabulary

division, repeated subtraction

$165 \div 5 = \boxed{}$

$126 \div 3 = \boxed{}$

$108 \div 4 = \boxed{}$

$204 \div 6 = \boxed{}$

2 Use repeated subtraction to complete these division calculations.

258 ÷ 6 =   152 ÷ 4 =

   258   152
–   60   10 × 6   –   40   10 × 4

3 Work out the answers to these word problems which involve a division calculation. Show your working clearly.

(a) There are 110 children in a tournament.
They are put into teams of 5.
How many teams are there?

_____ teams

(b) Egg boxes hold 6 eggs.
How many boxes are needed to pack 168 eggs?

_____ boxes

4 Find the missing number:

8 × ☐ = 400

Hint: Do not be confused by the × sign. You do not find the answer by multiplying.

Multiples and squares

Remember

Multiples are like numbers in the times tables but they go on and on, for example:

Multiples of 5 are: 5, 10, 15, 20 … 90, 95, 100, 105 …
Multiples of 9 are: 9, 18, 27, 36 … 90, 99, 108, 117 …

Square numbers are made by multiplying two identical whole numbers, for example

$4 \times 4 = 16$
16 is a square

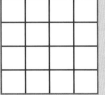

You will need: counters for activity 8

Vocabulary
multiple, square number

1   Complete this cross number puzzle.

Across		Down	
1	6×8	**1**	6×7
2	9×9	**3**	3×6
4	$24 \div 6$	**6**	6×6
5	$63 \div 7$	**7**	8×3
8	10×6		
9	7×2		

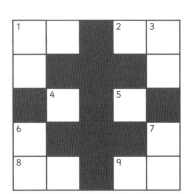

Design a crossword puzzle with multiplication and division problems as clues. Swap puzzles with your partner.

Hint: Try to memorise table facts. Knowing them really helps you in many ways.

2   Circle all the multiples of 8 in this list of numbers.

   28   32   56   58   72

Hint: Knowing table facts helps with questions of this type!

3   Complete this two-digit number so it is a multiple of 9.

   7

4   Write all the multiples of 6 that are greater than 30 and less than 60.

_____

5   Identify the number that satisfies all these clues.

   • It is under 20   • It is a multiple of 3   • It is a multiple of 5

Unit 1A: Number and problem solving
CPM framework 5Nc3, 5Nc5, 5Nc6; Teacher's resource 3.1, 4.1

6 Write these numbers in the correct places on the sorting diagram.

6   16   26   36

> **Hint:** This sorting diagram is also called a Venn diagram.

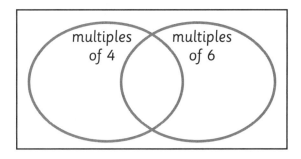

7 Complete the sequence of square numbers.

1, 4, 9, ☐, ☐, ☐, 49, ☐, ☐, 100

8 **Three in a line – a game for two players**

Each player could use counters of different colour, or you could cross out numbers on the game board.

Take turns to spin the spinner, square the number and put a counter on that number on one of the hexagons. Each player tries to make a line of four counters horizontally or diagonally. The winner is the first player to have four in a line.

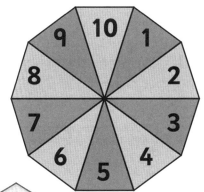

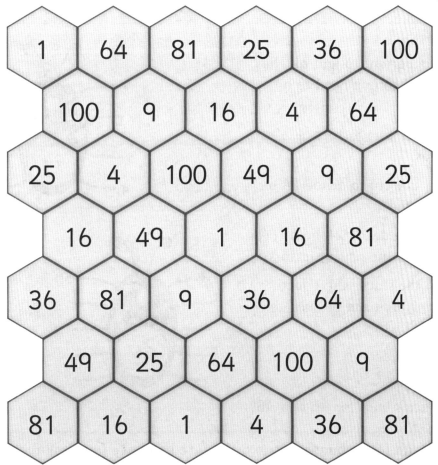

Unit 1A: Number and problem solving
CPM framework 5Nc3, 5Nc5, 5Nc6; Teacher's resource 3.1, 4.1

Factors and divisibility

Remember

Factors of a number divide exactly into the number.
They can be arranged in order or in pairs, for example:

Factors of 12: 1, 2, 3, 4, 6 and 12
Factors pairs for 12: 1 and 12, 2 and 6, 3 and 4

A number is **divisible** by:

100	if the last two digits are 00
10	if the last digit is 0
5	if the last digit is 0 or 5
2	if the last digit is 0, 2, 4, 6 or 8

You will need: resource 1,
page 80, for activity 5

Vocabulary
factor, multiple, divisible,
test of divisibility

1 Write the factors of these numbers, in order.

8 _____

9 _____

15 _____

2 Write the factors of these numbers, in pairs.

24 _____

28 _____

32 _____

3 Sometimes it is important to find **all** the factors of a number so you need to be systematic.

Here is a factor bug. The factors of 24 are written on its legs.

What happens if you try to divide 24 by 5? There is a remainder.

What happens if you divide 24 by 6? (You have already written the pair of factors.)

When you reach the stage where factor pairs are repeating, you can be sure you have found all the factors.

Now write them in order:
1, 2, 3, 4, 6, 8, 12, 24.

Now complete factor bugs for 36 and 45.

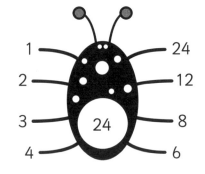

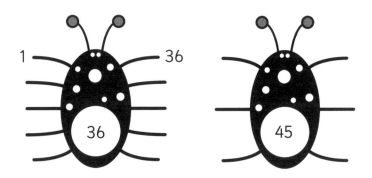

Hint: Working with factor bugs helps to make sure you have found all the factors.

Unit 1A: Number and problem solving, 4.2 Tests of divisibility, 4.3 Factors;
CPM framework 5Nc4, 5Nc7, 5Ps5

4 Circle three numbers that are divisible by 5.

101   102   103   104   105   106   107   108

109   110   111   112   113   114   115   116

> **Hint:** Numbers that are divisible by 5 are multiples of 5.

5 **Divisible – a game for two players**

Use a set of 0–9 digit cards from resource 1.
Take turns to pick three cards at random.
Use them to make a three-digit number.

If your number is divisible by 2, score 1 point.

If your number is divisible by 5, score 2 points.

If your number is divisible by 2 and 5 (or 10), score 3 points.

If your number is not divisible by 2, 5 or 10, score 0 points.

The first player to get 10 points is the winner.

Record your numbers here.

Player 1

| | | | Score | |

| | | | Score | |

| | | | Score | |

| | | | Score | |

| | | | Score | |

| | | | Score | |

| | | | Score | |

| | | | Score | |

| | | | Score | |

Player 2

| | | | Score | |

| | | | Score | |

| | | | Score | |

| | | | Score | |

| | | | Score | |

| | | | Score | |

| | | | Score | |

| | | | Score | |

| | | | Score | |

6 Shade the number that satisfies all these clues.

- is a multiple of 2
- is a multiple of 3
- is a factor of 12

| 1 | 2 | 3 | 4 | 5 | 6 | 7 | 8 | 9 | 10 |

> **Hint:** It is important not to confuse the words 'multiple' and 'factor'.

2D shapes and 3D solids

Remember

Equilateral triangles have three equal sides and three equal angles.
Isosceles triangles have two equal sides and two equal angles.
Scalene triangles have no equal sides.

equilateral triangle   isosceles triangle   isosceles right-angled triangle   scalene triangle   scalene right-angled triangle

Visualising 3D solids
Examples:

pyramid   triangular prism   tetrahedron   cube

You will need:
resource 2, page 81, for activity 2, resource 3, page 82, for activity 5, coloured pencils

Vocabulary
triangle, scalene, equilateral, isosceles, vertex, cube, face, pyramid, prism, tetrahedron, parallel, perpendicular

1 Making shapes

Draw two more lines to make an **isosceles** triangle.

Join three of the dots to make an **equilateral** triangle inside the regular hexagon.

Join three of the dots to make a **scalene** triangle inside the regular hexagon.

Hint: Use a ruler and make sure that you always draw the vertex of the triangle at a dot.

2 Triangle properties – games for two players

Play with a partner. You will find rules in the resources section on page 81.

Hint: Remember that an isosceles triangle and a scalene triangle may contain a right angle.

3 Draw a triangle with two perpendicular sides.

Hint: You cannot draw a triangle with two **parallel** sides.

Unit 1B: Geometry and problem solving
CPM framework 5Gs1, 5Gs4, 5Gs5, 5Pt5, 5Ps7; Teacher's Resource 5.1, 5.2, 28.1, 28.4

4 Parallel and perpendicular lines in shapes – a game for two players

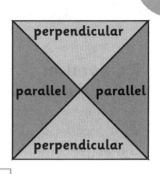

Players take turns to spin the spinner. If it lands on parallel (perpendicular) the player uses a ruler to colour over two parallel (perpendicular) lines in any one of the shapes. Play continues until all lines are used. If there are no more lines of the type you need, miss a turn. The player who has coloured more lines wins.

5 Cut out the eight nets for an open cube from resource 3. Use them to find out which square forms the base of the cube.

Colour the square that forms the base of the cube in each net.

> **Hint:** Each square is a face of the cube. The top is open.

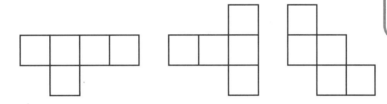

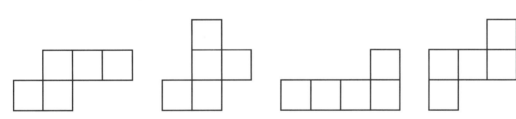

6 Look at items in the environment to find examples of different 3D solids.

Unit 1B: Geometry and problem solving
CPM framework 5Gs1, 5Gs4, 5Gs5, 5Pt5, 5Ps7; Teacher's Resource 5.1, 5.2, 28.1, 28.4

23

Translation and reflection

Remember

A **translation** moves an item in any direction. A translation is described as a number of units left or right and a number of units up or down.

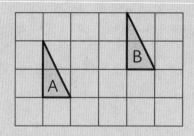

The translation moving shape A to shape B is 3 squares right and 1 square up

In a **reflection** a shape is flipped over a mirror line to face the opposite direction

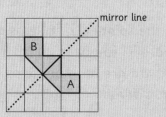

Shape A is reflected in the mirror line to shape B

Vocabulary
translation,
reflection,
mirror line

1 The quadrilateral is translated 3 squares to the right.

Draw the quadrilateral after it has been translated.

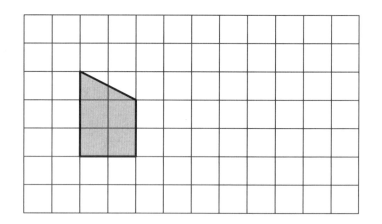

2 Here are some flags drawn on a coordinate grid.

(a) Flag A is translated 2 squares left and 4 squares up. Which shape will it reach? ☐

(b) Flag F is translated 1 square right and 6 squares up. Which shape will it reach? ☐

(c) Describe the translation which moves flag C to flag D. ☐

(d) Describe the translation which moves flag E to flag C. ☐

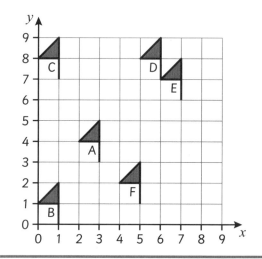

Hint: Write the movement left and right first and the movement up and down second.

Unit 1B: Geometry and problem solving
CPM framework 5Gp2, 5Gp3; Teacher's Resource 6.2

3 The shape is translated 2 squares right and 3 squares down.

Draw the new position of the shape.

Hint: Coordinates are explained on page 73.

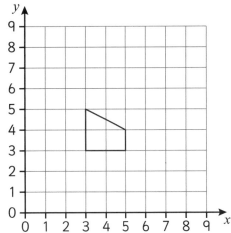

4 Draw the reflection of the pentagon in the mirror line.

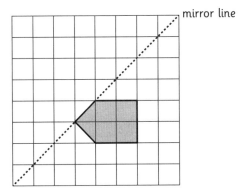

5 Draw the reflection of the hexagon in the mirror line.

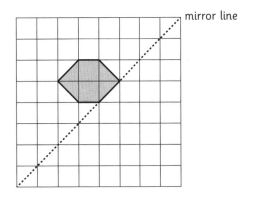

6 Shape A is drawn on a coordinate grid.

Reflect shape A in the mirror line.

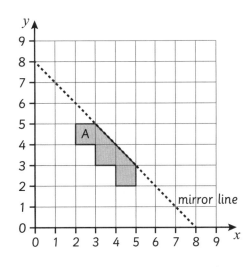

Time

Remember

These two clocks both show 10 minutes to nine.

analogue clock   digital clock

a.m. stands for ante meridiem which is in the morning.
p.m. stands for post meridiem which is in the afternoon

Timetables and many digital watches use the 24-hour clock

8:00 a.m. is written 08:00
8:00 p.m. is written 20:00

Time intervals

A film starts at 2:10 pm and lasts until 4:40 pm. How long does it last?

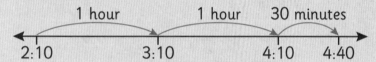

Use a time line to find the answer which is 2 hours 30 minutes.

You will need:
a pencil and paperclip to use the spinner, coloured pencils

Vocabulary
analogue, digital

1 Mia, Heidi and Katy take part in a race.

   • Mia finishes in 15 seconds.
   • Heidi finishes 4 seconds before Mia.
   • Katy finishes 3 seconds after Heidi

   How long does Katy take to finish the race? _____

Hint: Use a number line to help you distinguish between 'before' and 'after'.

2 Fill in the gaps in this table.

Seven o'clock in the evening	19:00	7:00 p.m.
Quarter to ten in the morning		
	14:20	
		3:15 p.m.

Hint: Beware: A common error when using 24-hour clock notation is to mistake the second digit of the hour time for the hour time so learners may think 14:00 is 4 o'clock.

Unit 1C: Measure and problem solving, Unit 2C: Measure and problem solving, Unit 3C: Measure and problem solving
CPM framework 5Mt1, 5Mt2, 5Mt4, 5Pt1, 5Ps1; Teacher's Resource 8.1, 20.1, 31.1

3 Look at the analogue clock.

Circle the correct time:

7:50   8:10   8:50   10:40

4 Look at the digital clock.

Which of these times is the same as that shown on the clock?

11:23 a.m.   3:13 p.m.   11:23 p.m.
2:23 p.m.   3:23 a.m.

5 The time is 5:30 p.m. Tick the clock that shows the wrong time.

6 Which of these times is equivalent to 4 o'clock in the afternoon?

4 a.m.   04:00   14:00   16:00

7 Cara puts a cake in the oven at 10:25.
It cooks for 40 minutes.

What time does it finish cooking?

> **Hint:** Remember there are 60 minutes in an hour. Try counting on in fives to 60, which will represent 11 o'clock.

8 Jamila went to her grandmother's house.

She arrived at 11:30 a.m. and left at 4:10 p.m.

How long was Jamila at her grandmother's house? _____

> **Hint:** Use a time line to help you answer the question.

9 Lucas visits a friend.
The clock shows the time as he arrives at his friend's home.

He leaves his friend's home at 8:50 p.m.

How long does he stay at his friend's home? _____

> **Hint:** This activity is a reminder that 18:00 and 8:00 p.m. do **not** represent the same time.

Unit 1C: Measure and problem solving, Unit 2C: Measure and problem solving, Unit 3C: Measure and problem solving
CPM framework 5Mt1, 5Mt2, 5Mt4, 5Pt1, 5Ps1; Teacher's Resource 8.1, 20.1, 31.1

27

Positive and negative numbers

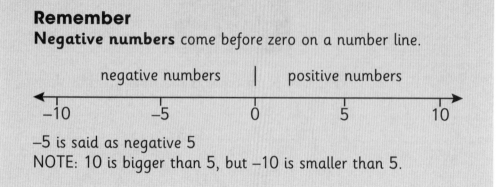

negative numbers | positive numbers

−10   −5   0   5   10

−5 is said as negative 5
NOTE: 10 is bigger than 5, but −10 is smaller than 5.

You will need: resource 4, pages 83–84, for activities 1 and 4

Vocabulary
positive number, negative number, zero

1 Ordering temperatures – a game for two players

Use a set of temperature cards and the recording sheet below.

The aim is to write the four temperatures in order, from lowest to highest.

Shuffle the cards and place them face down. Turn over the top card. Players look at the temperature on the card and choose which of their boxes to write it in.

Continue to fill in the other three boxes. The winner of the round is the player whose temperatures are written in order, or who has more numbers in the correct order.
Play 10 rounds.

Player 1   **Player 2**   **Winner**

Unit 2A: Number and problem solving, Unit 3A: Number and problem solving
CPM framework 5Nn9, 5Nn10, 5Pt1, 5Ps1; Teacher's Resource 11.1, 23.1

2 The table shows the average January temperatures in some cities.

Which is the coldest place?

_____

Which is the warmest place?

_____

Put the temperatures in order, lowest first.

_____

Place	Temperature (°C)
Beijing, China	−3
Budapest, Hungary	1
Delhi, India	14
Istanbul, Turkey	5
Karachi, Pakistan	18
Moscow, Russia	−8
Ulan Bator, Mongolia	−20

Hint: It is very cold in winter in Mongolia.

3 Complete the table.

Temperature now (°C)	Rise or fall in temperature	New temperature (°C)
2	A fall of 5 degrees	
−3	A rise of 8 degrees	
1	A fall of 5 degrees	
−4	A rise of 2 degrees	
6	A fall of 6 degrees	

The table shows the temperature in London on one day. Complete the table.

Place	Difference in temperature from London	Temperature (°C)
London		−1
Moscow		−25
New York	10 degrees lower	
Oslo	13 degrees lower	
Rio de Janeiro		26

4 Difference in temperature – a game for two players

Shuffle the temperature cards from resource 4 and spread them out face down.
Both players pick two cards each and work out the difference in temperature.
The player with the higher difference keeps their cards; the other player returns their cards.
Repeat until all the cards have been used. The winner is the player with more cards.

Record some of your pairs of cards.

Cards _____°C _____°C   Difference in temperature _____ degrees

Cards _____°C _____°C   Difference in temperature _____ degrees

Unit 2A: Number and problem solving, Unit 3A: Number and problem solving
CPM framework 5Nn9, 5Nn10, 5Pt1, 5Ps1; Teacher's Resource 11.1, 23.1

29

Decimals

Remember

Place value – the position of a digit in a number gives its value. The decimal point separates whole numbers from decimal places.

T	U	t	h
4	3	9	8

Read as forty-three point nine eight.

When **rounding** a decimal to the nearest whole number look at the tenths digit so 4.5 rounds up to 5.

When **comparing decimals**, look carefully at what zeros mean in decimal numbers.
These are all worth the same: 9   9.0   9.00
These are not worth the same: 9   0.9   0.09

You will need:
resource 5, page 85, for activity 1, resource 1, page 80, for activity 6, 2 dice

Vocabulary
decimal point, tenth, hundredth

---

1   Place-value match game – an activity for two players

Shuffle the cards from the resource and lay them face up on the table. Players take turns to find a matching trio, lay them side by side and read the two 'word cards' out loud.

An example of a matching trio:

4.61	four point six one	four units, six tenths and one hundredth

Write down two more examples.

> **Hint:** Always say decimals correctly:
> 4.51 is four point five one and not four point fifty one.

2   Place-value challenge – a game for two players

Use a dice or the spinner and a game board below.

Players take turns to roll the dice or spin the spinner and write their number in any cell on the game board. The winner is the player with the higher number when all the boxes have been filled.

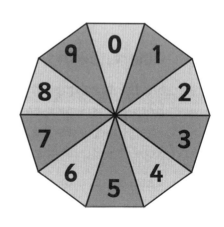

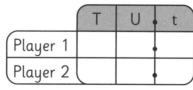

	T	U	t
Player 1			
Player 2			

Unit 2A: Number and problem solving, Unit 3A: Number and problem solving
CPM framework 5Nn4, 5Nn7, 5Nn11, 5Ps3; Teacher's Resource 11.1, 23.1

3 You have four cards: | **5** | **7** | **9** | **•** |

Which numbers can you make that are less than 100?

_____

4 Roll a dice two times and make a number with 1 decimal place.
Round to the nearest whole number.

Use the spinner for activity 2 if you do not have any dice.

2.5 rounds to 3.
5.2 rounds to 5.

Record four of your answers.

☐.☐ rounds to _____   ☐.☐ rounds to _____

☐.☐ rounds to _____   ☐.☐ rounds to _____

5 Decimal ladders – a game for two players

You will need two dice or the spinner from
activity 2 and this recording ladder with 7 rungs.

Players take turns to roll both dice and create a
decimal number, for example, with 1 and 3 you
could make 1.3 or 3.1. Place each number on a
rung so that all the numbers are in order with the
largest on top. The first player unable to go
loses the game.

Hint: There is space for seven numbers,
one on each rung of the ladder.

getting bigger

Unit 2A: Number and problem solving, **Unit 3A:** Number and problem solving
CPM framework 5Nn4, 5Nn7, 5Nn11, 5Ps3; Teacher's Resource 11.1, 23.1

6 Make the smallest number – a game for two to four players

Use two sets of 0–9 digit cards from the resource. Each player will need a decimal point card.

Shuffle the number cards and deal three cards to each player. The aim is for each player to make the smallest number, **greater than 1**, with their cards, for example if a player is dealt 0, 2 and 7 the smallest number they can make is 2.07. The winner is the first player to win five rounds.

Record your numbers:

cards   **smallest possible number**

☐ ☐ ☐   _____

☐ ☐ ☐   _____

☐ ☐ ☐   _____

☐ ☐ ☐   _____

☐ ☐ ☐   _____

Hint: You could play the game again but this time aim to make the largest possible number.

7 Use > or < to make this statement correct.

5.05 ☐ 5.5

Hint: Check the meaning of < and > on page 6.

8 Hassan has four number cards.

He chooses two cards.

He adds the numbers on the card together.

He rounds the result to the nearest whole number.

His answer is 5.

Which two cards did he choose?

Unit 2A: Number and problem solving, **Unit 3A:** Number and problem solving
CPM framework 5Nn4, 5Nn7, 5Nn11, 5Ps3; Teacher's Resource 11.1, 23.1

Multiplication strategies

Remember

Multiplication strategies

It is useful to learn some mathematical facts, such as multiplication facts up to 10 × 10.

You can use these facts to support your ability to work mentally, using strategies such as:

- multiplying by multiples of 10 and 100
- multiplying by 19 and 21
- multiplying by 25
- using factors to multiply.

Practise these strategies, using the examples in this unit.

You will need: Two sets of different coloured counters, or different coloured pens.

1 Three in a row – a game for two players

Use the spinner and some counters. Alternatively, you could cross through the numbers on the game board.

Players take turns to spin the spinner twice. Multiply the two numbers together and place a counter on the answer on the grid. If an incorrect answer is given, the other player can challenge and give the correct answer to claim the square. Once a square has been claimed it cannot be used again.

The first player to get three counters in a row is the winner.

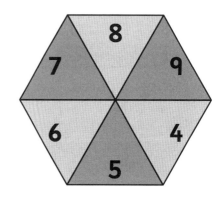

40	16	72	24	30	36
81	40	48	25	32	35
36	54	63	20	36	24
45	30	54	42	45	28
64	48	32	72	56	20
28	49	56	35	42	63

Hint: Games like this help to remember multiplication facts. Play them at home as often as you can.

Unit 2A: Number and problem solving, **Unit 3A:** Number and problem solving
CPM framework 5Nc3, 5Nc12, 5Nc13, 5Nc14, 5Nc15, 5Ps2; Teacher's Resource 12.2, 22.1

2 Multiply by multiples of 10 and 100.

> **Examples**
> $40 \times 9 =$
> $4 \times 9 = 36$
> so $40 \times 9 = 360$
>
> $700 \times 3 =$
> $7 \times 3 = 21$
> So $700 \times 3 = 2100$

Now try these.

$50 \times 7 =$

$400 \times 6 =$

$90 \times 8 =$

$300 \times 9 =$

3 To multiply a number by 19 or 21, multiply by 20 and add or subtract the number.

> **Examples**
> $13 \times 21 = (13 \times 20) + 13$
> $\qquad = 260 + 13$
> $\qquad = 273$
>
> $13 \times 19 = (13 \times 20) - 13$
> $\qquad = 260 - 13$
> $\qquad = 247$

Now try these.

11×19

11×21

4 To multiply by 25, multiply by 100, then divide by 4.

> **Examples**
> 39×25
> $39 \times 100 = 3900$
> $3900 \div 4 = 975$

Now try these.

13×25

17×25

5 Use factors.

> **Examples**
> $15 \times 6 = 15 \times 2 \times 3$
> $\qquad = 30 \times 3$
> $\qquad = 90$

Now try these.

13×6

15×8

Unit 2A: Number and problem solving, Unit 3A: Number and problem solving
CPM framework 5Nc3, 5Nc12, 5Nc13, 5Nc14, 5Nc15, 5Ps2; Teacher's Resource 12.2, 22.1

Doubling and halving

Remember
Doubling a two-digit number and deriving decimal facts

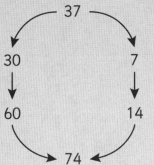

Double 37
Partition the number
into tens and units
double each part
separately
add the answers together

Deriving other facts

double 37 = 74

double 3.7 = 7.4
double 0.37 = 0.74

You will need:
resource 6,
page 86, for
activity 5

Vocabulary
double, half, halve,
inverse operations

Doubling multiples of 10 and 100 and deriving the corresponding halves
double 16 is 32 ⟶ double 160 is 320 ⟶ double 1600 is 3200
half of 32 is 16 ⟶ half of 320 is 160 ⟶ half of 3200 is 1600

Sharing
You can divide by 4 by halving and halving again.

Example:
20 cakes are to be divided among 4 people.
How many cakes does each person get?
$\frac{1}{2}$ of 20 = 10 $\frac{1}{2}$ of 10 = 5

Answer: 5 cakes
20 ÷ 4 can be worked out by halving 20 and then halving the result.

1 In these sequences of numbers, the rule is double the previous number.

Find the missing numbers in each sequence.

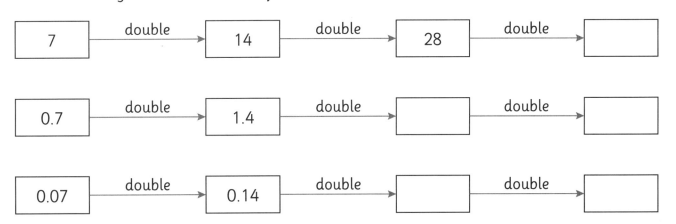

2 In this sequence each number is double the previous number.

Write in the missing numbers.

$\boxed{}$, $\boxed{}$, 4, 8, 16, $\boxed{}$, $\boxed{}$

> **Hint:** Doubling and halving are inverse operations
>
> $4 \xrightarrow{\text{double}} 8$
>
> $4 \xleftarrow{\text{halve}} 8$

3 Double 84 = 168

What is double 840? _____

> **Hint:** 840 is 10 × 84
> So the answer to double 840 is
> 10 × the answer to double 84.

What is double 8400? _____

Double 37 = 74

What is double 370? _____

What is double 3700? _____

4 Solve these problems by halving and halving again. Show your working.

(a) Ahmed shares $24 dollars among four people.

How much does each person get?

(b) Susanna shares 32 beads among four children.

How many beads does each child get?

5 Cut out the 12 jigsaw pieces from resource 6.

Reassemble by matching each calculation to its answer.

Stick down your pieces on the opposite page.

Unit 2A: Number and problem solving
CPM framework 5Nc16, 5Nc17, 5Nc25, 5Pt4; Teacher's Resource 12.3

Mental methods for addition and subtraction

You will need:
dice

Vocabulary
difference, multiple, near multiple

Remember

Counting on and back in 10s, 100s and thousands

- when counting in tens the units digit stays the same
- when counting in hundreds the tens and units digits stay the same
- when counting in thousands the hundreds, tens and units digits stay the same.

Adding and subtracting near multiples of 10, 100 and 1000

You may find it helpful to imagine, or draw, the numbers on a number line and then use strategies such as:

- $174 + 96 = 270$ because it is $174 + 100 - 4$ which is $274 - 4$
- $7003 - 1997 = 5006$ because it is $7003 - 2000 + 3$ which is $5003 + 3$

Calculating differences between near multiples of 100 or 1000:

Examples:
$405 - 297 = 108$

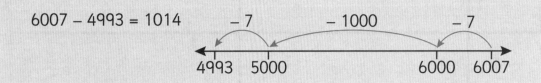

$6007 - 4993 = 1014$

1 Write the correct number in each empty box.

> **Hint:** Remember the units digit stays the same when counting forwards or backwards in tens.

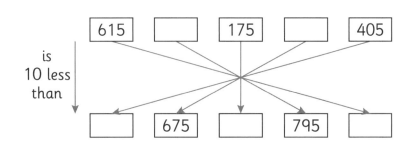

is 10 less than ↓

| 615 | | 175 | | 405 |

| | 675 | | 795 | |

2 Fill in the missing numbers in these sequences.

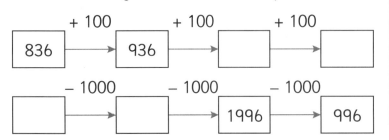

> **Hint:** Remember the tens and units digits stay the same when counting forwards or backwards in hundreds. Remember the hundreds, tens and units digits stay the same when counting forwards or backwards in thousands.

Unit 2A: Number and problem solving
CPM framework 5Nc8, 5Nc9, 5Nc10, 5Nc11; Teacher's Resource 13.3

3 Calculate:

234 + 97   234 – 97

2005 – 1999   1999 + 84

> **Hint:** Draw and use a number line to support working.

4 Finding the difference

Use a dice and a record sheet below.

(a) Using three-digit numbers

Roll the dice four times. Place the largest number in the first box and the other three numbers in any of the other three empty boxes to give a calculation such as 604 – 395. Work out the answer and record it. Make some different subtractions with your four numbers, remembering that the largest number must be in the first box.

Repeat with different numbers.

	0		–		9		=	
	0		–		9		=	
	0		–		9		=	
	0		–		9		=	

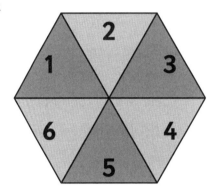

> **Hint:** Use a number line for support.

(b) Using four-digit numbers.

Repeat the activity, using this recording sheet.

	0	0		–		9	9		=	
	0	0		–		9	9		=	
	0	0		–		9	9		=	
	0	0		–		9	9		=	

5 Dicy darts – a game for two players

Each player starts with 301. Take turns to roll two dice or spin the spinner (from activity 4) twice. Make the largest two-digit number you can. Use a mental method to subtract this from your score. The first player to go below 100 wins.

> **Hint:** This game is an excellent way to practise mental calculation.

Collecting and representing data

Remember

You may need to collect **data** in order to answer a question or solve a problem. You may use a **tally chart**, a **data collection sheet** or you may conduct a survey.

When deciding what kind of chart or graph to use to **represent** your data, consider that:
- amounts that can take only certain values, such as whole numbers (discrete data) for different categories, are represented as **bar charts** or **bar line graphs**
- amounts that can take any value (continuous), such as temperature, are more logically expressed as a **line graph**.

1 Pierre wants to know how many cars pass school during 1 hour.

He draws tally marks to record the number of cars.

卌 卌 ||

How many cars pass the school? _____

Hint: Remember that tally marks are in blocks of 5.

卌 represents 5

2 Mia records information on the number of students attending a club.

Two of the entries in the table are missing.

Complete the table.

Session	Tally	Total
1	卌 |||	8
2	卌 ||	
3		9
4	卌		6

3 Sara sold fruit one day.

At the end of the day she says, 'I sold twice as many mangoes as peaches. I sold three times as many peaches as pineapples.'

Tick (✓) the table that represents the number of fruits Sara sold that day.

Mango	60
Peach	20
Pineapple	10

Mango	60
Peach	30
Pineapple	10

Mango	90
Peach	30
Pineapple	10

Mango	40
Peach	20
Pineapple	10

Unit 2B: Handling data and problem solving
CPM framework 5Dh1, 5Dh2, 5Ps5; Teacher's Resource 15.1

4 Yuri collected information about the colours of scooters.

Colour	Number of scooters
Red	8
Blue	12
Green	5
Black	3

The bar chart shows the information from his table.

Write in all the missing labels.

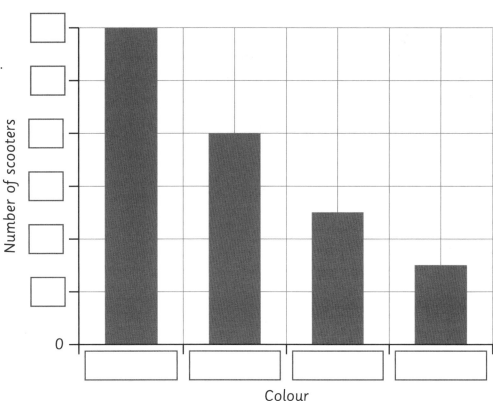

Number of scooters

Colour

5 Orla collected information about the number of sports played by some of her friends. She drew a table to show her results.

Sport	Number of friends
Netball	2
Rounders	6
Football	12
Cricket	15
Hockey	8

Draw two more lines to complete the bar line graph.

Hint: A bar line graph is similar to a bar chart, but lines (instead of bars) are used to show the information.

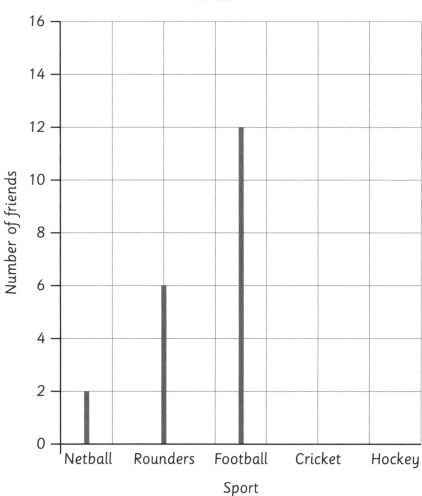

Number of friends

Netball   Rounders   Football   Cricket   Hockey

Sport

Interpreting data

Remember

When **interpreting data**, always read the key on a pictogram and the **scale** on a graph carefully. Remember that axes are not always labelled in ones.

Vocabulary

axis, axes, scale

In this pictogram, one drawing represents 2 cars.

White	🚗 🚗
Red	🚗 🚗 🚗
Blue	🚗 🚗
Silver	🚗 🚗 🚗 🚗

Key 🚗 represents 2 cars

In this bar chart, each square represents 5 matches.

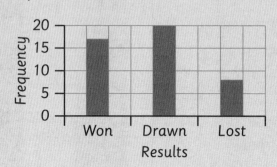

1   Ahmed, Chen, Hassan and Rajiv went on a treasure hunt. The graph shows the number of items each boy found.

How many items did they find altogether?

_____

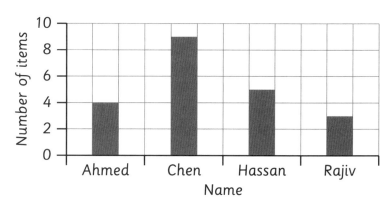

2   This graph shows when all the students in Class 5 and Class 6 have their birthdays.

   (a) How many students are there in Class 5 and Class 6 all together?

   _____

   The same numbers of students have birthdays in October, November and December.

   (b) How many students have a birthday in December?

   _____

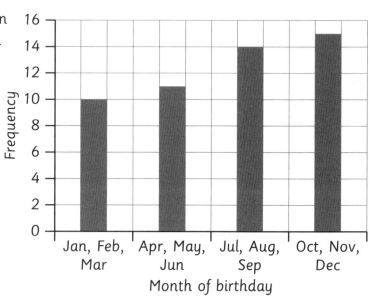

Hint: Remember to check the scale on the vertical axis.

Unit 2B: Handling data and problem solving
CPM framework 5Dh1, 5Dh2; Teacher's Resource 15.2

3 Angelique and Gabriella live in Australia and carried out a survey to find out students' favourite seasons.

They recorded the results on a bar line graph.

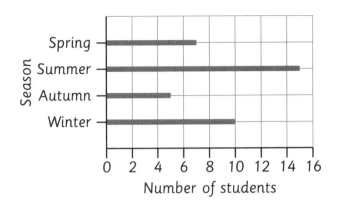

(a) How many more students chose summer than winter?

_____

(b) Angelique described her findings. She said, 'Twice as many students chose winter as chose autumn.'

Do you agree?

Explain your answer.

_____

(c) Write a sentence comparing the number of students who chose summer and those who chose autumn.

_____

4 The graph shows the favourite sports of a group of students.

Look at these four statements.

Which statement is true?

A Approximately 35 students chose swimming.

B Approximately three times as many students chose cycling than chose swimming.

C All the sports were chosen by more than 20 students.

D The number of students who chose sailing is approximately double the number who chose running.

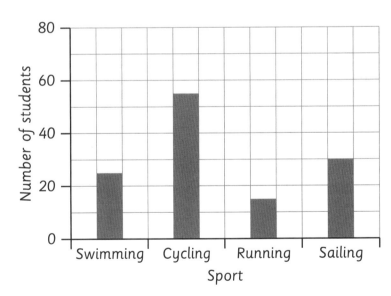

Hint: Work out your answer, then discuss it with a friend. Did you agree?

Probability

Remember

Probability is a measure of how likely it is that something will happen. Refer to the **probability scale**:

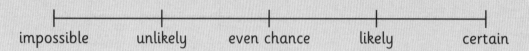

impossible   unlikely   even chance   likely   certain

1 Yuri uses a spinner shaped as a regular octagon.

Draw lines to show the probability that he spins each number.

The first one has been done for you.

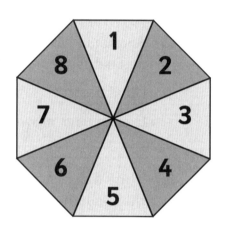

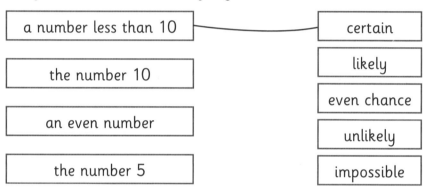

a number less than 10	—	certain
the number 10		likely
an even number		even chance
the number 5		unlikely
		impossible

2 Carlos has some bags containing black beads and white beads.

He takes a bead from a bag without looking.

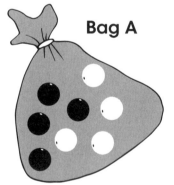 **Bag A**   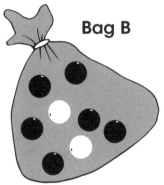 **Bag B**   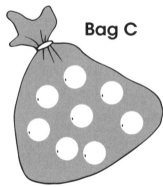 **Bag C**

Complete each statement.

(a) It is impossible for Carlos to take a black bead from bag _____ .

(b) It is unlikely that Carlos will take a white bead from bag _____ .

> **Hint:** You need to be familiar with the language of probability. Refer to the probability scale if you are unsure.

Unit 2B: Handling data and problem solving
CPM framework 5Db1; Teacher's Resource 16.1

3 **(a)** What is the probability of spinning a 2 on this spinner?

Draw a ring around the correct answer.

certain   impossible   even   likely   unlikely

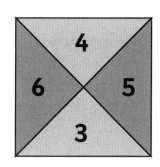

(b) What is the probability of spinning a number less than 10?

Mark your answer with an arrow (↓) on the probability scale.

```
├────────┼────────┼────────┼────────┤
impossible   unlikely   even chance   likely   certain
```

4 Ollie rolls a fair dice.

What is the probability that he rolls an even number? _____

What is the probability that he rolls an odd number? _____

What do you notice about your answers? Why is this? _____

_____

> **Hint:** Use the words given in activity 1 to help you.

5 Here are six number cards.

Mia picks a card without looking.

She finds the product of the two numbers on her card.

What is the most likely product? _____

> **Hint:** Look up the word 'product' if you can't remember the meaning.

6 This spinner is in the shape of a regular pentagon.

Write 1, 2 or 3 in each section of the spinner so that:

- 1 and 3 are equally likely to come up
- 2 is the least likely to come up

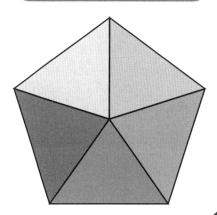

Line graphs

Remember

You can draw a line graph to show changes, for example, this one shows changes in temperature over time.

Fatima was ill during March. This graph is her temperature chart.

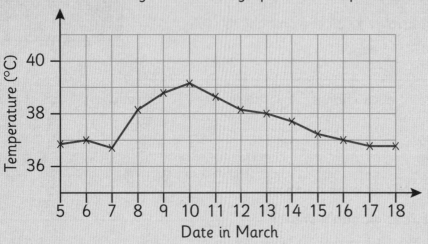

Intermediate points on a line graph may or may not have meaning. In this case, points are joined to show **trends**.

1 The graph shows how the temperature changed during part of a cold morning.

   What was the temperature at 9 am?

   _____

   At what time did the temperature reach 7°C?

   _____

   The temperature at 12 noon was 13°C. Mark this on the graph.

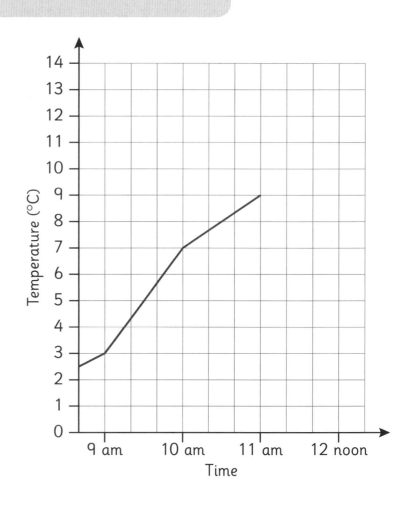

2 The graph shows Chen's cycle journey between 12 noon and 5 pm.

Here are four statements about his journey between 3 pm and 4 pm.

A He sat down to rest

B He read a book

C He went home

D He stopped to mend a puncture

One statement cannot be true.
Which one? _____

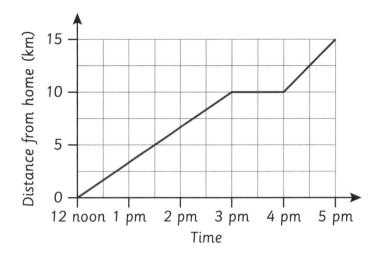

3 Here are two graphs showing the attendance in Class 5 during one week.

Graph A

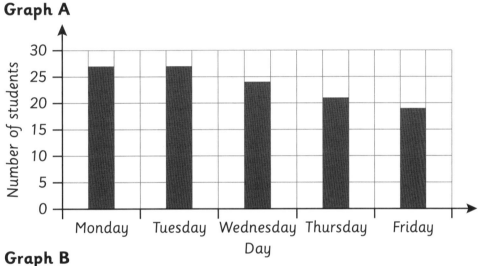

Graph B

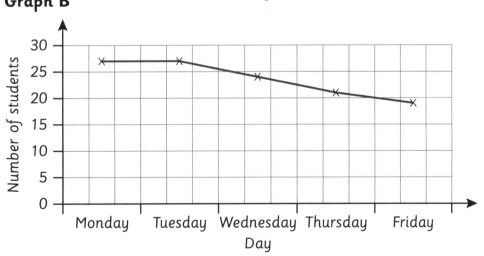

Graph B is not an appropriate way to show the information. Why not?

Finding the mode

Remember

The mode is the data item that occurs most often.

Example:

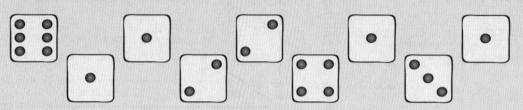

The mode is 1

1   The table shows the afternoon temperatures in London for
    seven days in spring.

Day	1	2	3	4	5	6	7
Temperature (°C)	21	23	18	11	11	12	13

What is the mode? _____

2   A dice was rolled 18 times.

Here are the results.

2   4   4   5   6   2   4   1   2

5   2   6   1   2   4   6   5   3

What is the mode? _____

> **Hint:** Draw a tally chart to help find the mode.

3   The table shows the distances, in kilometres, that Ali cycled on seven days.

Day	1	2	3	4	5	6	7
Distance (km)	22	47	26	33	47	12	13

What is the **modal** number of kilometres that Ali cycled each day?

_____

> **Hint:** Use the phrase **modal number of kilometres**.
> Treat this as the mode.

Unit 2B: Handling data and problem solving
CPM framework 5Dh5; Teacher's Resource 18.1 Finding the mode

4 Five friends went on a treasure hunt.

The graph shows the number of items each person found.

What was the modal number of items found?

_____

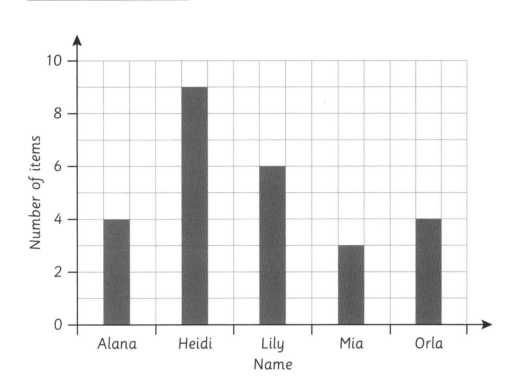

5 The table shows the numbers of days in each month.

Month	January	February	March	April	May	June	July	August	September	October	November	December
Number of days	31	28	31	30	31	30	31	31	30	31	30	31

Ollie says, 'The mode of the number of days in a month is 31.'

Is he right? Explain how you know.

_____

_____

6 Write a number in each of these boxes so that the mode of the five numbers is 10.

☐ ☐ ☐ ☐ ☐

Using scales, drawing and measuring lines

Remember

To find intermediate points when **reading a scale** find the difference between two marked points and divide by the number of spaces.

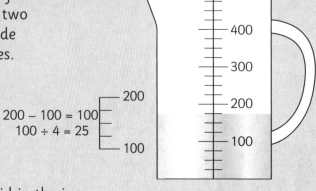

$$200 - 100 = 100$$
$$100 \div 4 = 25$$

There is 175 ml of liquid in the jug.

Vocabulary

units of length: metre (m), centimetre (cm), millimetre (mm)

units of mass: gram (g), kilogram (kg)

units of capacity: litre (l), millilitre (ml)

---

1 This jug contains some water.

Malik adds 150 millilitres of water to the jug.

Draw a line to show the new water level.

> **Hint:** The scale on this jug is the same as the one in the example.

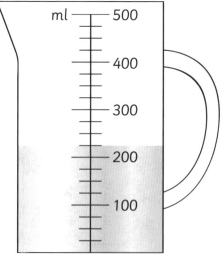

2 This 500 ml beaker contains some water.
The water is poured into another 500 ml beaker.

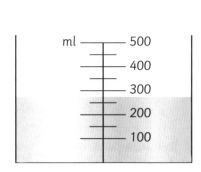

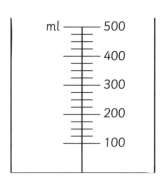

Draw a line on the diagram to show where the water would reach.

Unit 1C: Measure and problem solving, **Unit 2C:** Measure and problem solving, **Unit 3C:** Measure and problem solving
CPM framework 5MI1, 5MI5, 5MI6, 5MI7, 5Pt1, 5Ps1; Teacher's Resource 7.1, 19.1, 30.1

3 These dials are for measuring heavy masses. Draw an arrow to show each mass.

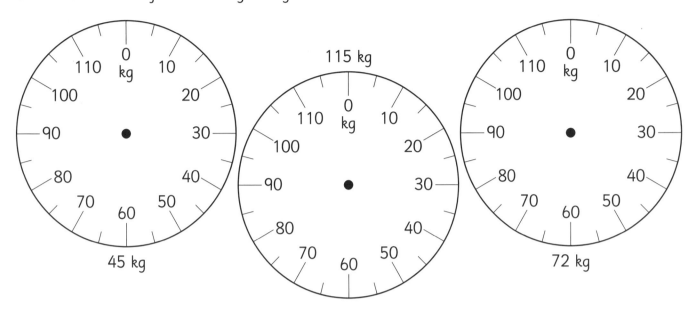

45 kg
115 kg
72 kg

4 Measure the length of the shortest side.

Give your answer to the nearest millimetre.

_____

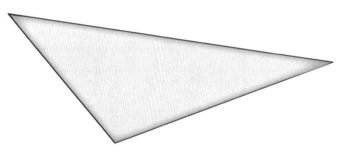

5 Drawing straight lines – an activity for two players

One player chooses a whole number of centimetres, up to 5. Both players estimate and draw a straight line, without using a ruler, as close to the chosen measurement as possible. Measure the lines and score 1 point if the measurement is within 1 cm of the target. Repeat for numbers 5–10, then 10–15 ... up to 30 cm. The player with the higher score after six rounds is the winner.

Record your lines below. Write your estimate and the measured length for each line.

Unit 1C: Measure and problem solving, **Unit 2C:** Measure and problem solving, **Unit 3C:** Measure and problem solving
CPM framework 5MI1, 5MI5, 5MI6, 5MI7, 5Pt1, 5Ps1; Teacher's Resource 7.1, 19.1, 30.1

51

Area and perimeter

Remember

The **perimeter** of a shape is the distance all around the edge.

The **area** is the amount of space covered.

This is the **formula for finding the area of a rectangle**.

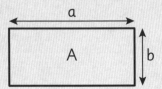

Area of a rectangle = length × width

$$A = a \times b$$

You will need:
squared paper,
a ruler

Vocabulary
area, perimeter

1   Draw letters on squared paper, like this, using horizontal and vertical lines only.

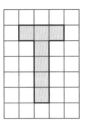

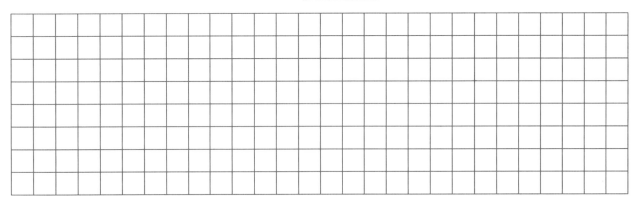

Work out the perimeter of the letters E, F, H, I, L and T.
Give your answers as a number of units.

Which letter has the smallest perimeter? _____   Which has the largest perimeter? _____

2   Here are four shapes on a grid.

Which two shapes have the

same **area**? _____

Hint: Area is usually measured in squares but it doesn't have to be. You can use other units, such as equilateral triangles and regular hexagons, that fit together.

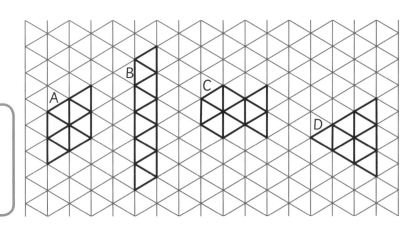

Unit 1C: Measure and problem solving, **Unit 2C:** Measure and problem solving, **Unit 3C:** Measure and problem solving
CPM framework 5Ma1, 5Ma2, 5Ma3; Teacher's Resource 9.1, 9.2, 21.1, 21.2, 32.1

3 Rory has some hexagonal tiles.
Each side is 2 cm long.

He puts two tiles together like this.

What is the **perimeter** of his shape?

_____

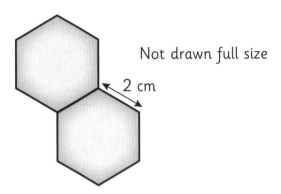

Not drawn full size

2 cm

4 What is the **perimeter** of a rectangle
6 cm long and 4 cm wide?

_____

What is the **area** of the rectangle?

_____

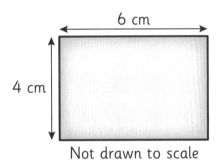

6 cm

4 cm

Not drawn to scale

5 This rectangle is twice as long as it is wide.

What is the **perimeter** of the rectangle?

_____

What is the **area** of the rectangle?

_____

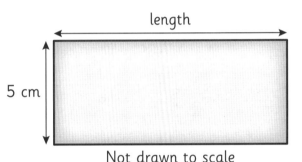

length

5 cm

Not drawn to scale

> **Hint:** Find the length of the longer side first.

6 Find the area of each rectangle.

(a) length 7 cm, width 6 cm   _____

(b) length 4 cm, width 9 cm   _____

(c) length 5 cm, width 8 cm   _____

Find the area of each square.

(d) side 8 cm   _____

(e) side 7 cm   _____

(f) side 9 cm   _____

> **Hint:** Use the formula for finding the area.

Unit 1C: Measure and problem solving, **Unit 2C:** Measure and problem solving, **Unit 3C:** Measure and problem solving
CPM framework 5Ma1, 5Ma2, 5Ma3; Teacher's Resource 9.1, 9.2, 21.1, 21.2, 32.1

53

Percentages

Remember

Per cent means 'out of 100'.

50% is $\frac{50}{100} = \frac{1}{2}$

10% is $\frac{10}{100} = \frac{1}{10}$

To **find a percentage** of a quantity, express the percentage as a fraction, multiply the quantity by the fraction.

Example: Find 10% of 350

$10\% = \frac{1}{10}$

$350 \div 10 = 35$

1 Write down the percentage that is shaded in.

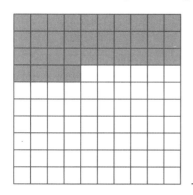   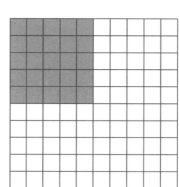

Hint: Remember that 1% is $\frac{1}{10}$.

2 Shade 10% of each of these grids.

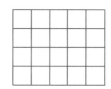   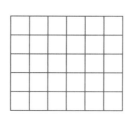

3 Write these fractions as percentages.

$\frac{35}{100} = $ _____ $\frac{36}{100} = $ _____ $\frac{72}{100} = $ _____ $\frac{14}{100} = $ _____ $\frac{67}{100} = $ _____

4 Write these fractions as percentages.

$\frac{3}{10} = $ _____ $\frac{7}{10} = $ _____ $\frac{9}{10} = $ _____

Hint: $\frac{1}{10} = 10\%$.

5 $\frac{1}{4} = \frac{25}{100}$

What is $\frac{3}{4}$ as a percentage? _____

Unit 3A: Number and problem solving
CPM framework 5Nn19, 5Nn20, 5Ps2, 5Ps9; Teacher's Resource 24.1

6 Write the percentage of each shape that is shaded.

 _____

 _____

 _____

7 Maria looks at the label in her coat. Part of it is missing.

What percentage is cashmere? _____

80% Wool
% Cashmere

Hint: 100% is a whole.

8 Join each box to the correct amount.

50% of 20

10% of 180

100% of 14

14

12

10

16

18

20

9 Here are two apple trees.
Tree A produces 40 kg of apples.
Tree B produces 50% more than tree A.

How many kilograms of apples does tree B produce?

Working:

Tree B produces 40 kg + 50% of 40 kg

50% of 40 kg =

Tree B produces 40 +

Hint: Use this working box as a template for other similar questions.

10 A shop sells a bicycle for $200. The same bicycle is sold on the internet for 10% less.

What is the cost of the bicycle on the internet?

Working:

Price on internet is $200 − 10% of $200

10% of $200 =

Price on internet = $200 −

Equivalent fractions, decimals and percentages

Equivalent fractions are equal in value, for example $\frac{1}{2} = \frac{2}{4} = \frac{4}{8}$.

You normally write the fraction with the smallest possible denominator, referred to as the **simplest form**.

- To order and compare fractions change them all to equivalent fractions with the same denominator.
- To order and compare fractions, decimals and percentages change them all to one type, usually all to decimals.

Example:
Order the following starting with the smallest: $\frac{7}{10}$, 50%, 0.6.

$\frac{7}{10} = 0.7$ and $50\% = 0.5$ so the order is: 50%, 0.6, $\frac{7}{10}$

You will need: resource 7, page 87, for activity 3

Vocabulary
numerator, denominator, equivalent fraction

1 Use these number lines to help you complete the table of equivalent fractions, decimals and percentages.

Hint: Try to learn these equivalences.

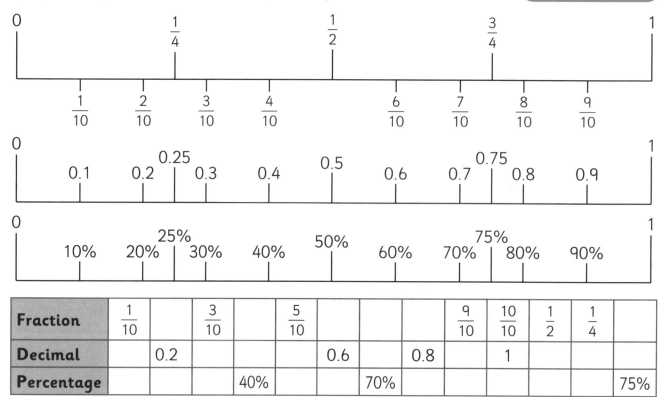

Fraction	$\frac{1}{10}$		$\frac{3}{10}$		$\frac{5}{10}$				$\frac{9}{10}$	$\frac{10}{10}$	$\frac{1}{2}$	$\frac{1}{4}$	
Decimal		0.2				0.6		0.8		1			
Percentage				40%			70%						75%

2 Complete these equivalent fractions.

$\frac{3}{4} = \frac{6}{}$

$\frac{4}{5} = \frac{}{15}$

$\frac{2}{5} = \frac{}{25}$

3 Three of a kind – a game for two to four players

Use the 18 playing cards from resource 7. Shuffle the cards and deal three cards to each player. If anyone has 'three of a kind', for example, $\frac{1}{2}$, 50% and 0.5, they score 3 points, anyone with 'two of a kind' scores 2 points. Otherwise it is a draw. Return the cards and shuffle again.
Repeat until someone has 10 points.

Record two different combinations that scored 3 points.

Hint: The game will reinforce the work done in activity 1. It is much harder to match when the values are not in order.

4 Match each fraction to the equivalent percentage.
One has been done for you.

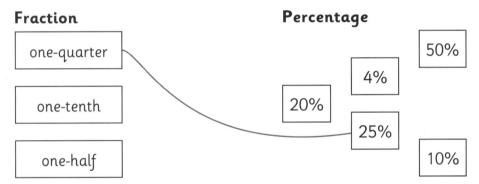

Fraction

one-quarter

one-tenth

one-half

Percentage

50%

4%

20%

25%

10%

5 Circle **two** fractions that are equivalent to 0.4.

$\frac{4}{10}$ $\frac{1}{40}$ $\frac{40}{100}$ $\frac{1}{4}$

6 Write these fractions, decimals and percentages in order of size, starting with the smallest.

$\frac{2}{10}$ 0.5   40%   0.25

Hint: Change them all to one type, decimals or percentages. Do not choose fractions because it is not possible to compare fractions with different denominators.

7 Put these numbers in order starting with the smallest.

0.6 $\frac{1}{2}$ $\frac{65}{100}$ 0.55

smallest _____ _____ _____ _____ largest

Mixed numbers and improper fractions

Remember

A **whole number** can be written as a fraction, for example, $\frac{1}{1}, \frac{2}{2}, \frac{3}{3}$.

$1\frac{2}{3}$ is a **mixed number** because it is made up of a whole number and a fraction.

$\frac{5}{3}$ is the equivalent **improper fraction**, because the numerator is larger than the denominator.

You can change an improper fraction to a mixed number.

Example: $\frac{17}{5}$

Find out how many whole numbers there are by division $17 \div 5 = 3$ remainder 2

That is 3 whole ones and two-fifths written as $3\frac{2}{5}$

Vocabulary

improper fraction, mixed number, numerator, denominator

1 Convert these improper fractions to mixed numbers.

$\frac{9}{4}$ $\qquad$ $\frac{12}{5}$ $\qquad$ $\frac{16}{3}$ $\qquad$ $\frac{37}{10}$

2 Place these numbers in order, smallest first.

$\frac{1}{2}$ $\qquad$ $1\frac{1}{2}$ $\qquad$ 2 $\qquad$ $\frac{1}{4}$ $\qquad$ $1\frac{3}{4}$

> **Hint:** A number line like the one in Activity 3 may be helpful.

3 Join each improper fraction to the correct position on the number line.

> **Hint:** Change the improper fractions to mixed numbers first.

$\frac{7}{4}$ $\qquad\qquad\qquad\qquad$ $\frac{5}{2}$ $\qquad\qquad\qquad\qquad$ $\frac{6}{3}$

Unit 3A: Number and problem solving
CPM framework 5Nn17; Teacher's Resource 24.3

4 Complete the number line – a game for two players.

Use the spinner and recording sheet below.

- Players take turns to use the spinner to give two numbers.

- Arrange the numbers so the larger one is the numerator, for example 3 and 5 would give $\frac{5}{3}$.

- Change the improper fraction into a mixed number: $\frac{5}{3} = 1\frac{2}{3}$

- Find the number on one of the number lines and initial the square next to it.

- If the two numbers are the same you will get a whole number, not a mixed number.

- Continue playing until one player has initialled all the boxes on both lines. That player is the winner.

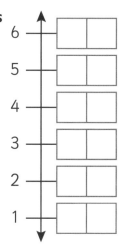

Mixed numbers

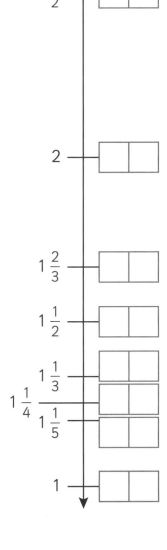

Whole numbers

	Whole numbers	Mixed numbers
	$\frac{1}{1}, \frac{2}{2}, \frac{3}{3}, \frac{4}{4}, \frac{5}{5}$ and $\frac{6}{6} = 1$	$\frac{6}{5} = 1\frac{1}{5}$
	$\frac{2}{1}, \frac{4}{2}$ and $\frac{6}{3} = 2$	$\frac{5}{4} = 1\frac{1}{4}$
	$\frac{3}{1}$ and $\frac{6}{2} = 3$	$\frac{4}{3} = 1\frac{1}{3}$
	$\frac{4}{1} = 4$	$\frac{6}{4}$ and $\frac{3}{2} = 1\frac{1}{2}$
	$\frac{5}{1} = 5$	$\frac{5}{3} = 1\frac{2}{3}$
	$\frac{6}{1} = 6$	$\frac{5}{2} = 2\frac{1}{2}$

Addition and subtraction of decimals

Remember

Decimal facts

Derive quickly decimals (tenths) with a total of 1, for example:

$0.7 + 0.3 =$ ☐ and $1 - 0.7 =$ ☐

$0.1 +$ ☐ $= 1$ and $1 - 0.1 =$ ☐

Derive quickly decimals (ones and tenths) with a total of 10, for example:

$3.7 + 6.3 =$ ☐ and $10 - 3.7 =$ ☐

$8.5 +$ ☐ $= 10$ and $10 - 8.5 =$ ☐

Addition and subtraction of money

On pages 10–11 you worked with addition and subtraction of whole numbers. The method can be extended to working with money.

Addition: $367 + 185$ and $\$3.67 + \$1.85$

```
  3 6 7                3.6 7
+ 1 8 5              + 1.8 5
  4 0 0  300 + 100     4 0 0  3 + 1
  1 4 0  60 + 80       1 4 0  0.6 + 0.8
    1 2  7 + 5           1 2  0.07 + 0.05
  5 5 2                5.5 2
```

Subtraction: $365 - 122$ and $\$3.65 - \$1.22$

```
 300  + 60  + 5        3 + 0.6 + 0.05
- 100    20    2      - 1   0.2   0.02
 200  + 40  + 3        2 + 0.4 + 0.03
```

---

1 Complete the spider diagram so that numbers on opposite ends add up to 1.

2 Write in the missing numbers so each line adds up to 1.

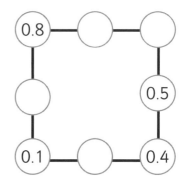

3 Fill in the missing numbers.

$0.8 + 0.2 =$ ☐ $0.3 +$ ☐ $= 1$ ☐ $+ 0.5 = 1$

Unit 3A: Number and problem solving
CPM framework 5Nc1, 5Nc2, 5Nc19, 5Ps3; Teacher's Resource 23.1, 25.1

4 Complete the spider diagram so that numbers on opposite ends add up to 10.

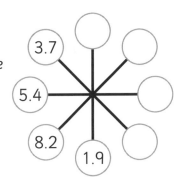

5 Fill in the missing numbers.

6.8 + 3.2 = ☐

7.3 + ☐ = 10

☐ + 9.5 = 10

6 Here are four digit cards.

Use each digit once to make two two-digit numbers that total 10.

☐.☐ + ☐.☐ = 10

7 Calculate:

4.5 + 2.8 = _____   7.8 – 3.5 = _____

2.9 + 3.6 = _____   6.2 – 5.7 = _____

8 Highest score – a game for two players

Use a 1–6 dice or the spinner and the recording sheet below.

Roll the dice or spin the spinner. Each player writes the number in one of their boxes. Repeat five more times until all the boxes are filled. Add the numbers. The player with the higher answer wins 1 point. The first player to win three rounds is the champion.

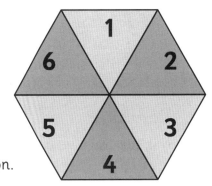

Player 1

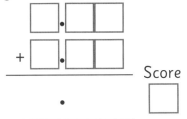 Score ☐

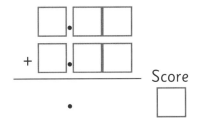 Score ☐

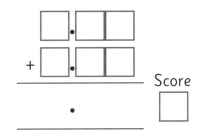 Score ☐

Player 2

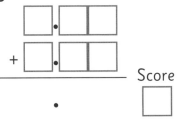 Score ☐

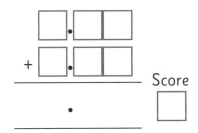 Score ☐

Score ☐

Division and working with remainders

Remember

You need to make sensible decisions about rounding up or down after division. For example, $240 \div 52$ is 4 remainder 32, but whether the answer should be rounded up to 5 or down to 4 depends on the context.

Example of **rounding down**:
I have 240 cakes. One box holds 52 cakes.
I could fill only 4 boxes of cakes

Example of **rounding up**:
There are 240 people. One bus holds 52 people.
5 buses are needed to hold all the people

Fractions and division

Finding one third is equivalent to dividing by 3,
so $\frac{1}{3}$ of 15 is equivalent to $15 \div 3$.

When 3 whole cakes are divided equally into 4 each person gets three quarters of a cake, or $3 \div 4 = \frac{3}{4}$.

Be aware that $\frac{12}{3}$ is another way of writing $12 \div 3$.

You will need:
resource 8, page 88, for activity 7

Vocabulary
remainder, rounding down, rounding up, equivalent, equally

1   Shade the divisions that have a remainder in the answer.

What letter have you made? _____

> **Hint:** Knowing table facts helps to answer questions like this quickly and accurately. There is more practice with tables on pages 18–19 and 33–34.

$40 \div 3$	$32 \div 3$	$40 \div 6$
$16 \div 6$	$30 \div 6$	$32 \div 8$
$36 \div 8$	$29 \div 9$	$62 \div 10$
$28 \div 9$	$36 \div 9$	$28 \div 4$
$46 \div 5$	$30 \div 7$	$24 \div 5$

2   Sometimes you need to express a remainder as a fraction, for example:

$15 \div 2 = 7$ remainder 1 $15 \div 2 = 7\frac{1}{2}$ ← remainder
← number you are dividing by

$19 \div 4 = 4$ remainder 3 $19 \div 4 = 4\frac{3}{4}$ ← remainder
← number you are dividing by

Write these divisions in the same way.

$20 \div 3 =$ $16 \div 5 =$

Unit 1A: Number and problem solving, Unit 3A: Number and problem solving
CPM framework 5Nn18, 5Nc24, 5Nc26, 5Pt7, 5Ps10; Teacher's Resource 3.4, 25.2

3 Work these out. Show your working and how you deal with any remainder.

(a) Plastic cups are sold in packets of 8.
Milly needs 28 cups. How many packs must she buy?

(b) 36 children need 2 pencils each.
There are 20 pencils in a box. How many boxes are needed?

(c) Sara puts 4 seeds in each pot.
She uses 5 pots and has 1 seed left over. How many seeds did she start with?

(d) A box holds 6 eggs.
Ahmed has 50 eggs. How many boxes can he fill?

(e) Conrad saves $2 each week.
How many weeks does he need to save to buy a book costing $18.25?

4 **(a)** What is $\frac{1}{4}$ of $16?

> **Hint:** To find $\frac{1}{4}$ divide by 4.

(b) What is $\frac{3}{4}$ of $16?

5 **(a)** What is $\frac{1}{3}$ of $12?

(b) What is $\frac{2}{3}$ of $12?

Unit 1A: Number and problem solving, Unit 3A: Number and problem solving
CPM framework 5Nn18, 5Nc24, 5Nc26, 5Pt7, 5Ps10; Teacher's Resource 3.4, 25.2

63

6 Divide the rectangle into four parts.
They must be $\frac{1}{2}$, $\frac{1}{4}$, $\frac{1}{6}$ and $\frac{1}{12}$ of the rectangle.
The pieces must not overlap.

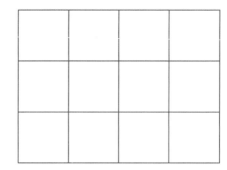

7 Collecting fraction cards – a game for two players

Cut out the cards from resource 8.

Shuffle the cards and lay them face down on the table. Take turns to spin the spinner and choose a card. If the spinner shows the answer to the card, keep the card; if not, replace the card in its original position. If you spin a 0 you can choose any card, say the answer and keep the card.

The winner is the player with the most cards when all the cards have been chosen.

Look at the cards in your pile.

Write down one calculation to give each of these answers.

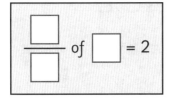

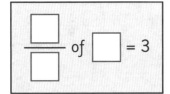

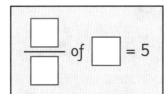

Unit 1A: Number and problem solving, Unit 3A: Number and problem solving
CPM framework 5Nn18, 5Nc24, 5Nc26, 5Pt7, 5Ps10; Teacher's Resource 3.4, 25.2

Using inverse operations and brackets

Remember

Inverse operations

Operations that, when combined, leave the number on which they operate unchanged.

This idea is useful when finding missing numbers in calculations of these types:

Addition and subtraction are inverse operations

$6 + \boxed{} = 25$ so $25 - 6 = \boxed{}$

Multiplication and division are inverse operations

$3 \times \boxed{} = 24$ so $24 \div 3 = \boxed{}$

Using brackets

When part of a calculation is in **brackets**, work out the brackets first.

Vocabulary

inverse operation, brackets

1 Fill in the missing numbers.

$\boxed{} + 38 = 100$ $\boxed{} \div 4 = 8$

$83 - \boxed{} = 28$ $7 \times \boxed{} = 63$

2 Fill in the missing numbers.

$50 + 30 = 100 - \boxed{}$ (**Hint:** Work out $50 + 30$ first.) $150 - 90 = \boxed{} + 40$

3 Write numbers in the boxes to make this calculation correct.

$50 - \boxed{} = \boxed{} + 20$

Hint: There are many different answers.
How many whole number answers can you find?

4 Complete the multiplication grid.

Hint: Multiplication and division are inverse operations. To find the number in the box on the top row you could use:

$\boxed{} \times 5 = 45$ or $\boxed{} \times 4 = 36$ or $\boxed{} \times 2 = 18$

×	7	5	
5		25	45
4	28		36
2	14	10	18

5 Number machines

Look at the number machine below.

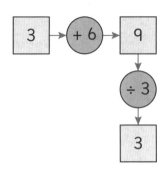

Make up some puzzles for a friend to try.

> **Hint:** Put in all the numbers and operations, then rub out the ones you want your friend to work out. Make sure it is possible to do!

Now write the four missing numbers in this number machine.

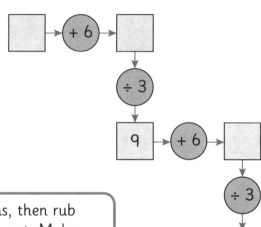

6 Complete these calculations.

$(13 - 8) + 4 =$ $(20 - 4) + 5 =$

$15 - (5 - 2) =$ $(15 - 7) + 3 =$

$16 - (7 + 2) =$ $16 + (13 - 8) =$

7 Draw brackets to make each answer 10.

$14 - 10 + 6$ $20 - 5 - 5$

$11 - 6 - 5$ $19 - 14 + 5$

8 Use these numbers to complete the calculations: 2, 3, 4, 5.

$20 - (\boxed{} + 9) = 7$ $11 - (\boxed{} - 3) = 9$

$(9 + \boxed{}) - 3 = 8$ $(11 - \boxed{}) + 2 = 10$

9 Use these numbers, any of the operations (=, −, × or ÷) and brackets to make number statements that give the target answer:

2, 3 and 4   Target 2

2, 6 and 30   Target 7

3, 8 and 12   Target 12

Make up some similar puzzles for a friend to do.

Unit 3A: Number and problem solving
CPM framework 5Nc27, 5Pt3; Teacher's Resource 25.3

Ratio and proportion

Remember

A **ratio** compares **part to part**.
For every grey square, there are 3 white squares.

A **proportion** compares **part to whole**. It can be given as a fraction, as a decimal or as a percentage. 'What proportion?' means 'What fraction?', or 'What decimal?', or 'What percentage?'

Example:
There are 4 squares altogether.

1 out of 4 squares is grey ($\frac{1}{4}$, 0.25, 25%).

3 out of 4 squares are white ($\frac{3}{4}$, 0.75, 75%).

1   Here is a recipe for vegetable soup.

The recipe is enough for 4 people. To make enough for 8 people, you need to double the amount of each ingredient, for example, you would need 300 g × 2 = 600 g of potatoes.

Work out the quantities of these ingredients:

	For 4 people	For 8 people
butter beans		
stock		
mushrooms		
tomatoes		
pumpkin		

Vegetable soup
(serves 4 people)

1 large onion
300 grams potatoes
650 grams butter beans
350 ml stock
2 carrots
250 grams mushrooms
400 grams chopped tomatoes
850 grams pumpkin

2   Nour makes a birthday cake for 20 children. The recipe she uses gives quantities for five people. Complete the table to show the amounts Nour uses.

Ingredients	For 5 children	For 20 children
flour	600g	
sugar	400g	
butter	450g	
eggs	3	

3 Here is a string of dark and light beads.

What fraction of the beads are dark? _____

> **Hint:** This is often the way questions on proportion are presented.

4 Bead patterns – a proportion game for two players

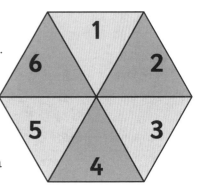

Take turns to roll the dice or spin the spinner to give two numbers. Arrange them in order, smallest first, for example 2 and 3.

Try to match the numbers with the proportion of beads on the record sheet, for example player 1 could match 2 and 3 with the first row and say '2 in every 3 beads are light'. If the player can match their numbers to a bead pattern they write the statement in the box.

The winner is the first player to match all their rows.

Player 1

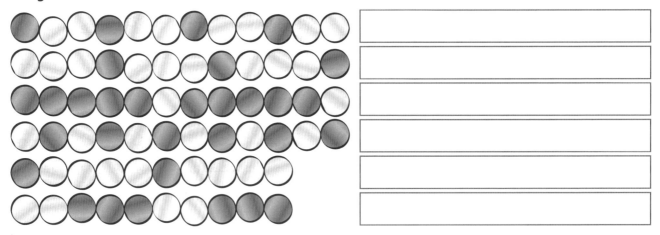

Player 2

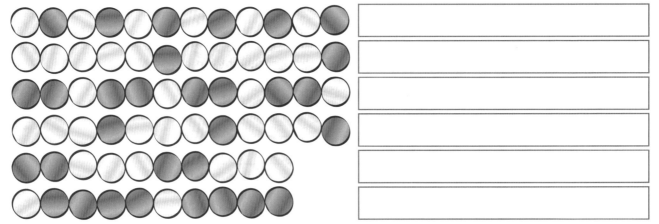

Unit 3A: Number and problem solving
CPM framework 5Nn21, 5Nn22; Teacher's Resource 26.1

Angles

Remember
There are different types of angle.

a straight line is 180°

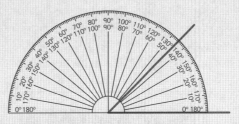

90° is a right angle

acute angles are less than 90°

obtuse angles are more than 90°

You use a **protractor** to measure angles.

When using a protractor ensure that the protractor is positioned correctly.
Do **not** place the edge of the protractor on one of the arms of the angle.
Always count round from 0°.

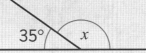

The **sum of the angles on a straight line** is 180°.

$x = 180° - 35° = 145°$

35° x

You will need: a protractor

1 Measure each angle. Use a protractor.

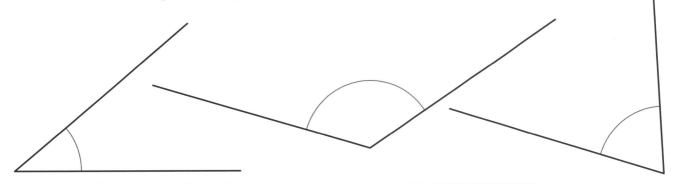

> **Hint:** Look at the angle to decide whether it is acute or obtuse, then look at your answer and ensure that it matches the type of angle.

2 Write **acute** or **obtuse** by each angle.

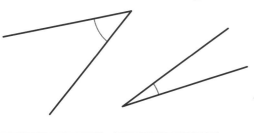
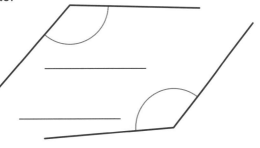

Unit 1B: Geometry and problem solving, Unit 3B: Geometry and problem solving
CPM framework 5Gs6, 5Gs7; Teacher's Resource 5.1, 27.1

69

3 Angles – a game for two players

Start with a straight line then draw two more lines meeting at a point.

Each person writes down their estimates of each of the three angles. Measure the angles. Score 2 points if you are within 10° and 1 point if you are within 5° of the agreed measure of each angle. The first to 15 points is the winner.

Record your results below.

Estimates		Angle 1	Angle 2	Angle 3
	Player 1			
	Player 2			

Estimates		Angle 1	Angle 2	Angle 3
	Player 1			
	Player 2			

Estimates		Angle 1	Angle 2	Angle 3
	Player 1			
	Player 2			

Estimates		Angle 1	Angle 2	Angle 3
	Player 1			
	Player 2			

4 This is a pentagon drawn on a square grid.

Complete the sentence.

This pentagon has _____ acute angles

and _____ obtuse angles.

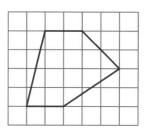

5 Calculate the size of the angle marked x.

20° x $x =$ _____ °

$x =$ _____ ° 155° x

$x =$ _____ ° 110° x

Hint: The sum of the angles on a straight line is 180°.

Unit 1B: Geometry and problem solving, **Unit 3B:** Geometry and problem solving
CPM framework 5Gs6, 5Gs7; Teacher's Resource 5.1, 27.1

Symmetry

Remember

If a shape has **reflective symmetry**, a **line of symmetry** divides it in half. One half is a **reflection** of the other. The line of symmetry is often called the **mirror line**.

Some shapes have no lines of symmetry and other shapes have more than one line of symmetry.

2 lines of symmetry

1 line of symmetry

0 lines of symmetry

A shape or pattern has **rotational symmetry** if when it is turned around its centre point it matches the original outline more than once.

An equilateral triangle has rotational symmetry order 3

This design has rotational symmetry order 4

You will need: resource 9, page 89, a brass fastener for activity 3

Vocabulary
symmetry, reflection, mirror line, rotation

1. Shade in two more squares so the design is symmetrical in both mirror lines.

2. Colour the octagon to make a design that is symmetrical about the two mirror lines.

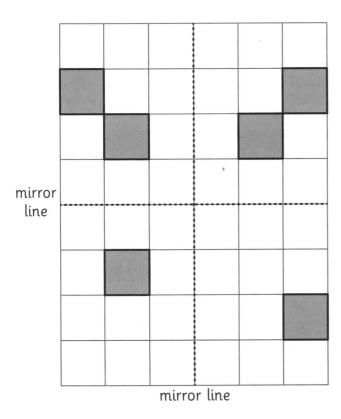

mirror line

mirror line

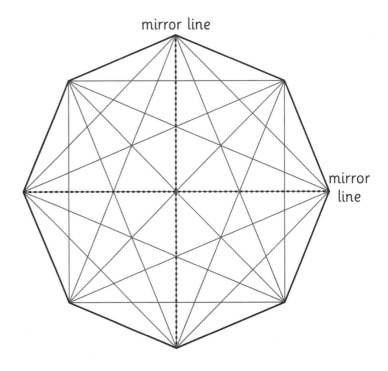

mirror line

mirror line

mirror line

3 Use resource 9 and a brass fastener.

Complete each instruction on a separate diagram.

- Join every second dot to form a regular hexagon
- Join every third dot to form a square
- Join every fourth dot to form an equilateral triangle

Trace and cut out the shapes, then fold to find all the lines of symmetry. Can you see a pattern relating the number of sides and the number of lines of symmetry? Record your results.

regular hexagon

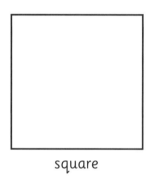
square

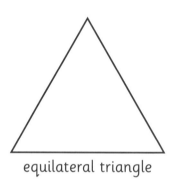
equilateral triangle

I notice that _____

Using the same shapes, explore rotational symmetry by placing two identical shapes on top of one another then fixing a brass fastener in the centre and turning the top shape. Can you see a pattern relating to the number of sides and the order of rotational symmetry?

I notice that _____

> **Hint:** A regular polygon has equal sides and equal angles.

4 Complete this table.

	equilateral triangle	square	regular pentagon	regular hexagon
number of lines of symmetry				
order of rotational symmetry				

> **Hint:** This only happens when the shapes are regular!

Unit 3B: Geometry and problem solving
CPM framework 5Gs2, 5Gs3; Teacher's Resource 28.2, 28.3

Coordinates and transformations

Remember

Know the convention that the **coordinates** (2, 1) describe a point found by starting from the origin (0, 0) and moving two across and one up.

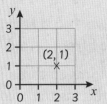

In a **reflection**, a shape is flipped over a mirror line to face the opposite direction. Shape A is reflected in the mirror line to shape B

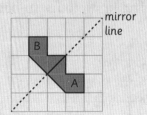

A **translation** moves an item in any direction.
A translation is described as a number of units left or right and a number of units up or down.
The translation moving shape A to shape B is 3 squares right and 1 square up.

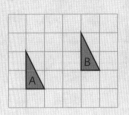

You will need: 2 dice for activity 3

Vocabulary
coordinates, axis, reflection, translation

1 Three points, A, B and C, are marked on a grid.

What are the coordinates of these points?

_____

A, B and C are three vertices of a rectangle.
What are the coordinates of the fourth vertex?

_____

> **Hint:** One vertex but many vertices.
> The exact position of the point is marked with a cross.

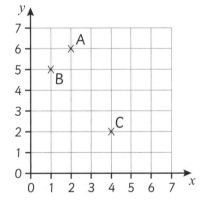

2 Draw the reflection of each shape in the mirror line.

> **Hint:** It may be easier to draw the reflection if you turn the page so the mirror line is vertical.

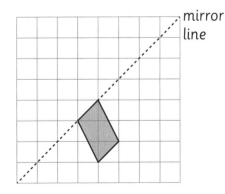

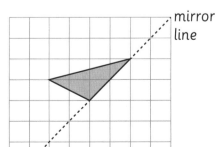

Unit 1B: Geometry and problem solving, **Unit 3B:** Geometry and problem solving
CPM framework 5Gp1, 5Gp2, 5Gp3; Teacher's Resource 6.1, 6.2, 29.1

73

3 Four in a row coordinates – a game for two players

Use two 1–6 dice and the coordinate grids below with the x and y axes marked from 0 to 6.

Take turns to throw both dice. Choose one score as the x coordinate and the other as the y coordinate. Mark this point on your grid with a cross. The first player to get four crosses to form a line is the winner.

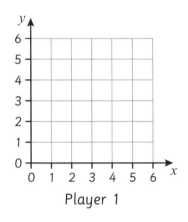
Player 1

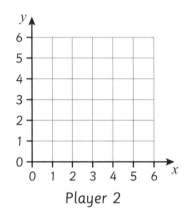
Player 2

4 Draw the new position of the rectangle after it has been translated 4 squares to the right and 2 squares down.

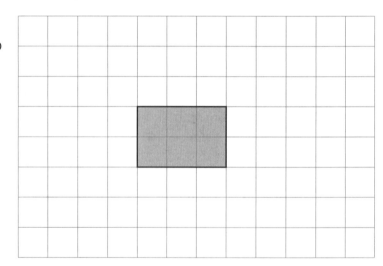

5 Describe the translation that moves square A to square B.

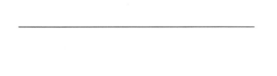

_____

_____

Unit 1B: Geometry and problem solving, **Unit 3B:** Geometry and problem solving
CPM framework 5Gp1, 5Gp2, 5Gp3; Teacher's Resource 6.1, 6.2, 29.1

Length, mass and capacity

Remember

Converting larger to smaller units
Use a place-value chart to help you,
for example:
1 kg = 1000 g so 2.6 kg = 2600 g

Th	H	T	U	t
			2	6
2	6	0	0	0

You will need:
resource 10,
page 90, for
activity 1,
a ruler

Ordering measurements in mixed units
Change all the measurements to the same unit before you try to order
them, for example:
Order 20 cm, 1 m, 30 mm and 2.5 cm starting with the smallest.
1m = 100 cm and 30 mm = 3 cm
So ordering smallest to largest is: 2.5 cm, 30 mm, 20 cm, 1m

Rounding measurements to the nearest whole unit
Example: a 3.25 kg bag of carrots weighs 3 kg to the nearest kilogram
(See pages 30–32).

1   Measures dominoes – a game for two players

Use the 18 dominoes cut from the resource.

- Place each domino face down on the table.

- Each player chooses nine dominoes.

- The player with the domino showing 1 kilometre places this on the table.

- Players then take turns to match one of their end points to those laid.

For example:

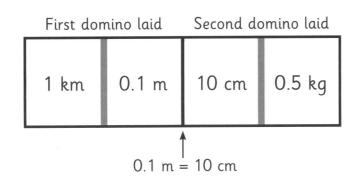

First domino laid   Second domino laid

| 1 km | 0.1 m | 10 cm | 0.5 kg |

The next player must
match a domino to
1 km or 0.5 kg

0.1 m = 10 cm

- A player who is unable to go misses that turn.

- Play continues until one player has laid all their dominoes.

Hint: This game provides practice in using important conversions.
Players could work on their own and use the dominoes to make a loop.

Unit 1C: Measure and problem solving, **Unit 3C:** Measure and problem solving
CPM framework 5MI1, 5MI2, 5MI3, 5MI4, 5Pt1, 5Ps1; Teacher's Resource 7.1, 30.1

75

2 Tick (✓) the sentences that could be true.

☐ Zina's pencil is 15 cm long

☐ Heidi is 15 m tall

☐ Petra's younger sister weighs 15 kg

☐ Fatima's water bottle holds 15 l

> **Hint:** Look at labels on cartons, tins and bottles to check how much they hold.

3 Complete the table showing the mass of some fruits.

	Mass in grams	Mass in kilograms
A watermelon		2
Bag of apples		1.4
Bag of cherries		0.5

> **Hint:** 1000 g = 1 kg
> To change kilograms to grams, multiply by 1000

4 Ingrid has a piece of ribbon 1 metre long.

She cuts off a piece 40 cm long.

How many centimetres of ribbon remain?

_____

> **Hint:** 100 cm = 1 m

5 Ali is 1.5 metres tall.

Chen is 1.2 metres tall.

How many centimetres taller is Ali than Chen?

_____

> **Hint:** To change metres to centimetres multiply by 100.

Unit 1C: Measure and problem solving, **Unit 3C:** Measure and problem solving
CPM framework 5MI1, 5MI2, 5MI3, 5MI4, 5Pt1, 5Ps1; Teacher's Resource 7.1, 30.1

6 Bashir needs to put 2 litres of water in a bucket.

He has a 500 ml jug.

How can he measure 2 litres of water?

_____

7 Write these lengths in order of size starting with the shortest.

55 mm   5 cm   5 m   55 cm

_____

Hint: 1000 ml = 1 litre

> **Hint:** Change all the measurements to the same unit before you attempt to order them.
> 10 mm = 1 cm

8 Write these masses in order of size staring with the lightest.

2 kg   200 g $\frac{1}{2}$ kg   0.25 kg

_____

9 Measure the length of the diagonal of the rectangle.

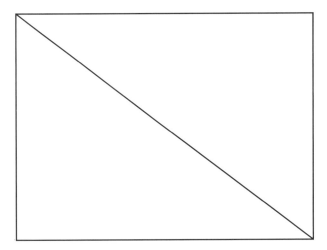

Write your answer in millimetres.   _____

Write your answer in centimetres.   _____

10 What is 1.65 metres to the nearest metre?   _____

Write 1.275 litres to the nearest litre.   _____

Write 1.509 kilograms to the nearest kilogram.   _____

> **Hint:** Think of 1.65 on a number line between 1 and 2. Is 1.65 closer to 1 or to 2?

Unit 1C: Measure and problem solving, **Unit 3C:** Measure and problem solving
CPM framework 5MI1, 5MI2, 5MI3, 5MI4, 5Pt1, 5Ps1; Teacher's Resource 7.1, 30.1

77

Using timetables and calendars

Remember

Here is part of a **timetable**. Times are shown using the 24-hour clock.

Newtown	12:16	14:16
Hightown	12:58	14:58
Shortstown	13:38	15:35

Vocabulary
timetable, calendar

You need to know the number of days in each month of the year. You can look at a **calendar**, but learning this rhyme may help you to remember these facts:

30 days hath September,
April, June and November.
All the rest have 31,
except in February alone
which has but 28 days clear
and 29 in each leap year.

1 Here is part of the morning timetable for Class 6.

10:30	10:45	11:30	12:15	1:30
	Break	Maths	Science	Lunch

(a) How long does the maths lesson last? _____

(b) What time does the afternoon session start? _____

(c) How long is it from the end of break to the start of lunch?

_____

2 Here is part of a bus timetable.

(a) Pierre catches the 3:30 p.m. bus at Hightown. How long does it take him to travel to Shortstown?

Newtown	12:16	14:16	14:46	16:16
Hightown	12:58	14:58	15:30	16:58
Shortstown	13:38	15:35	16:16	17:36

_____

(b) Manjit travels from Newtown to Shortstown. She arrives at the bus stop at half past 2. Which bus will she catch?

_____

What time will she arrive in Shortstown?

_____

Hint: Remember to use time lines to work out time intervals. Look back at pages 26–27 for a reminder.

Unit 1C: Measure and problem solving, **Unit 2C:** Measure and problem solving, **Unit 3C:** Measure and problem solving
CPM framework 5Mt3, 5Mt5, 5Mt6; Teacher's Resource 8.2, 20.2, 31.1

3 A cycling competition starts on 6th December and runs for exactly two weeks.

When does the competition **end**?

_____

4 Angelique goes to dancing class every Wednesday. She goes to the class on Wednesday 1st July.

How many dancing classes does she go to in July?

_____

5 Here is a calendar for August 2000.

Sanjiv was born on 29th July 2000.

On what day of the week was he born?

_____

6 Use a calendar for this year to answer these questions.

(a) Which months start on a Saturday?

_____

(b) Which months end on a Friday?

_____

(c) How many Sundays are there in July?

_____

(d) Write the date of your birthday. Which day of the week is your birthday on?

_____

(e) A cycling club meets on the first Tuesday of each month. Write the dates of all the meetings.

_____

Unit 1C: Measure and problem solving, **Unit 2C:** Measure and problem solving, **Unit 3C:** Measure and problem solving
CPM framework 5Mt3, 5Mt5, 5Mt6; Teacher's Resource 8.2, 20.2, 31.1

79

9	8	7
6	5	4
3	2	1
0	•	0
1	2	3
4	5	6
7	8	9

Photocopiable resources

Resource 2
Triangle properties – games for 2 players

Cut out the 16 cards. There are some repeats.

Game 1

Shuffle the cards and place them face down in a pack. Take turns to pick up one card. Both players draw a triangle that fits the description. Compare your drawings.

Game 2

Shuffle cards and lay them face down, spread all over the table. Players take turns to turn over two cards. If they can draw a triangle that satisfies **both** properties, they win the pair of cards. Otherwise the cards are put back where they were and play passes to the next player. If, towards the end of the game, the players are convinced that there are no more possible pairs they can stop the game, turn the cards over and discuss whether they were correct.

Has only one line of symmetry	Has just two equal sides	Contains a right angle	Contains a right angle but does not have a line of symmetry
Has all its sides equal	Has all its angles equal	All its sides are of different length	All its angles are of different sizes
Contains a right angle	Contains a right angle and has two equal sides	All its sides are of different length	Contains a right angle and has all its sides of different length
Has three lines of symmetry	Does not contain a right angle	Has no line of symmetry	Does not contain a right angle

Resource 3
Nets of open cubes

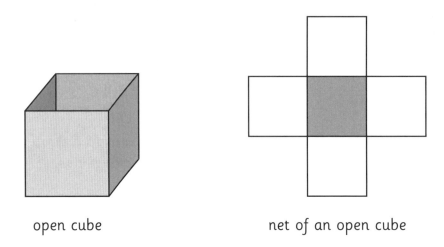

open cube   net of an open cube

Here are the nets of 8 open cubes. Colour the square that forms the base of the open cube.

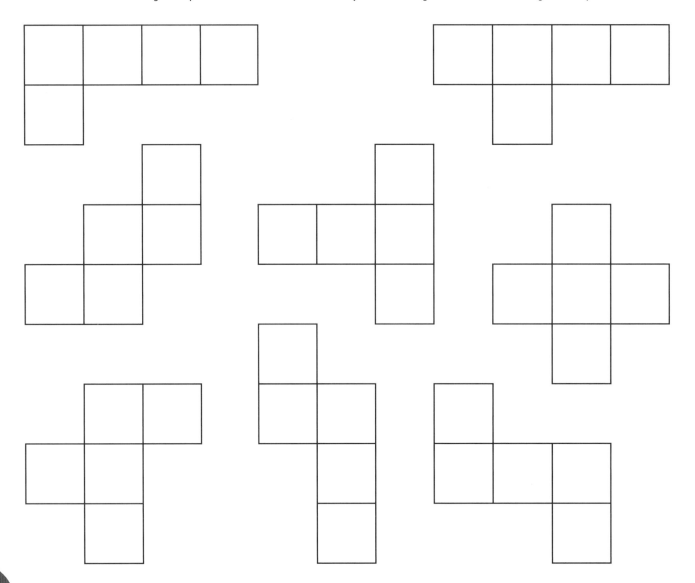

Resource 4
Temperature cards

Cut out the cards.

10°C	9°C	8°C
7°C	6°C	5°C
4°C	3°C	2°C
1°C	0°C	−1°C
−2°C	−3°C	−4°C
−5°C	−6°C	−7°C
−8°C	−9°C	−10°C

Cut out the cards.

20°C	19°C	18°C
17°C	16°C	15°C
14°C	13°C	12°C
11°C		−11°C
−12°C	−13°C	−14°C
−15°C	−16°C	−17°C
−18°C	−19°C	−20°C

Resource 5
Decimal place-value match

Cut out the cards.

4.61	four point six one	four units, six tenths and one hundredth
0.05	zero point zero five	five hundredths
9.19	nine point one nine	nine units, one tenth and nine hundredths
0.7	zero point seven	seven tenths
5.09	five point zero nine	five units and nine hundredths
45.7	forty five point seven	four tens, five units and seven tenths
7.4	seven point four	seven units and four tenths
7.0	seven	seven units
7.04	seven point zero four	seven units and four hundredths
0.5	zero point five	five tenths

Cut out the 12 jigsaw pieces. Reassemble by matching each calculation to its answer.

Double 39 — Half of 86 / 43	Half of 94 — Double 46 / 92	Double 26
78 / Double 49 — Half of 68	47 / 98 — Double 19	52 / Half of 28 — 14 / Half of 96
34 / Half of 90 — Double 36	38 / 45 — Half of 72	48 / Double 47 — 94 / Double 29
72 / Double 23	36 / 46	58 / Half of 62 — 31

Cut out the 18 cards.

$\dfrac{1}{2}$	50%	0.5
$\dfrac{1}{10}$	10%	0.1
$\dfrac{1}{4}$	25%	0.25
$\dfrac{3}{10}$	30%	0.3
$\dfrac{7}{10}$	70%	0.7
$\dfrac{3}{4}$	75%	0.75

Resource 8
Collecting fraction cards
– a game for 2 players

Cut out the 20 cards.

$\frac{1}{2}$ of 4	$\frac{1}{2}$ of 6	$\frac{1}{2}$ of 8	$\frac{1}{2}$ of 10
$\frac{1}{2}$ of 12	$\frac{1}{3}$ of 6	$\frac{1}{3}$ of 9	$\frac{1}{3}$ of 12
$\frac{1}{3}$ of 15	$\frac{1}{3}$ of 18	$\frac{1}{4}$ of 8	$\frac{1}{4}$ of 12
$\frac{1}{4}$ of 16	$\frac{1}{4}$ of 20	$\frac{1}{4}$ of 24	$\frac{1}{5}$ of 10
$\frac{1}{5}$ of 15	$\frac{1}{5}$ of 20	$\frac{1}{5}$ of 25	$\frac{1}{5}$ of 30

Photocopiable resources

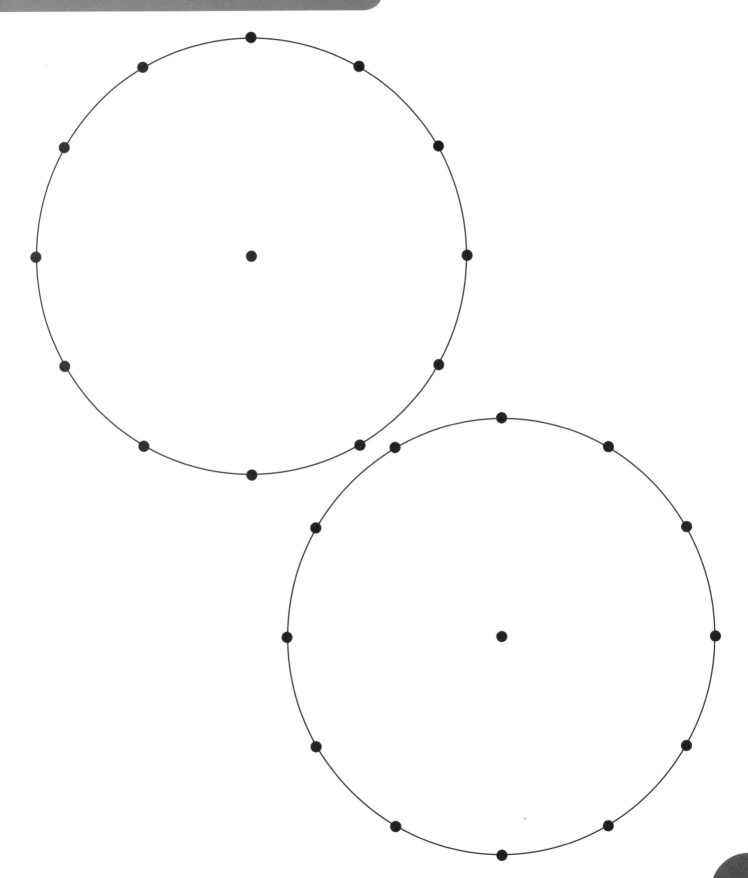

Photocopiable resources

Resource 10
Measure dominoes

Cut out the 18 dominoes.

1 km	0.1 m	10 cm	0.5 kg	500 g	0.75 l
750 ml	0.25 km	250 m	0.1 l	100 ml	4 kg
4000 g	1 kg	1000 g	5000 ml	5 l	0.25 l
250 ml	0.75 m	75 cm	5 m	500 cm	2000 m
2 km	0.25 kg	250 g	1 m	100 cm	0.5 km
500 m	7 cm	70 mm	0.5 m	50 cm	1000 m

Answers

Page 4 Place value

1 ninety thousand

2 (a) 97531

(b) 13579

(c) ninety seven thousand five hundred and thirty one

thirteen thousand five hundred and seventy nine

3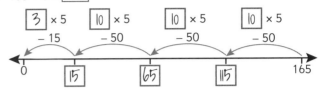

5

IN	3489	864	45 678	37 902	18 700	1870
OUT	34 890	8640	456 780	379 020	187 000	18 700

IN	54 800	864 000	45 100	902 000	18 700	187 000
OUT	548	8640	451	9020	187	1870

Page 6 Ordering and rounding

1 < > <

> > <

4

	rounded to the nearest 100
456	500
4562	4600
45 628	45 600
456 281	456 300

5 3778

3762, 3772, 3778, 3779, 3781, 3783, 3819, 3826

Page 8 Sequences and general statements

1 Start at the 2 and count in threes.

1	2	3	4	5
6	7	8	9	10
11	12	13	14	15
16	17	18	19	20
21	22	23	24	25

Start at the 1 and count in threes.

1	2	3	4	5
6	7	8	9	10
11	12	13	14	15
16	17	18	19	20
21	22	23	24	25

Start at the 3 and count in fours.

1	2	3	4	5	6
7	8	9	10	11	12
13	14	15	16	17	18
19	20	21	22	23	24
25	26	27	28	29	30
31	32	33	34	35	36

2 add 3

3 6, 2, −2

4 circle 120, 230, 30 and 1000

Page 10 Addition and subtraction

3 191, 519

Page 12 Multiplication by a single digit

1 (a) 114, 11.4

(b) 245, 24.5

Page 16 Division

1 165 ÷ 3 = 33

126 ÷ 3 = 42

104 ÷ 8 = 27

204 ÷ 6 = 34

2 43, 38

3 (a) 22 teams

(b) 28 boxes

4 50

Page 18 Multiples and squares

1

1 4	8		2 8	3 1
2				8
		4 4	5 9	
6 3				7 2
8 6	0		9 1	4

2 32, 56, 72

3 72

4 36, 42, 48, 54

5 15

6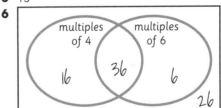

7 16, 25, 36 and 64, 81

Page 20 Factors and divisibility

1 1, 2, 4, 8

1, 3, 9

1, 3, 5, 15

2 1 and 24, 2 and 12, 3 and 8, 4 and 6

1 and 28, 2 and 14, 4 and 7

1 and 32, 2 and 16, 4 and 8

3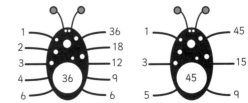

4 105   110   115

6

1	2	3	4	5	6	7	8	9	10

Answers

Page 22 2D shapes and 3D solids

1 Many different answers including:

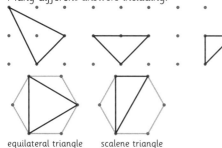

equilateral triangle   scalene triangle

3 Check that learner's drawings are right-angled triangles

5

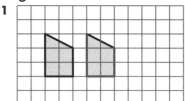

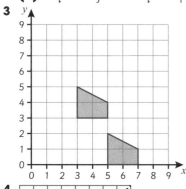

Page 24 Transition and reflection

1

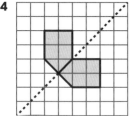

2 (a) C

(b) D

(c) 5 squares right

(d) 6 squares left and 1 square up

3

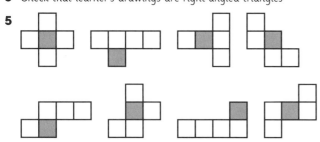

4

5

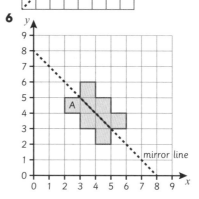

6

Page 26 Time

1 14 seconds

2

Seven o'clock in the evening	19:00	7:00 p.m.
Quarter to ten in the morning	09:45	9:45 a.m.
Twenty minutes past two in the afternoon	14:20	2:20 p.m.
Quarter past three in the afternoon	15:15	3:15 p.m.

3 7:50

4 11:23 p.m.

5

6 16:00

7 11:05

8 4 hours 40 minutes

9 2 hours 45 minutes

Page 28 Positive and negative numbers

2 Ulan Bator

Karachi

−20, −8, −3, 1, 5, 14, 18

3

Temperature now (°C)	Rise or fall in temperature	New temperature
2	A fall of 5 degrees	−3°C
−3	A rise of 8 degrees	5°C
1	A fall of 5 degrees	−4°C
−4	A rise of 2 degrees	−2°C
6	A fall of 6 degrees	0°C

Answers

Place	Difference in temperature from London	Temperature (°C)
London		−1
Moscow	24 degrees lower	−25
New York	10 degrees lower	−11
Oslo	13 degrees lower	−14
Rio de Janeiro	27 degrees warmer	26

Page 30 Decimals
3 57.9, 59.7, 75.9, 79.5, 95.7, 97.5, 5.79, 5.97, 7.59, 7.95, 9.57, 9.75

7 5.05 < 5.5

8 1.4 and 3.4

Page 33 Multiplication strategies
2 350, 720, 2400, 2700

3 209, 231

4 325, 425

5 78, 120

Page 35 Doubling and halving
1
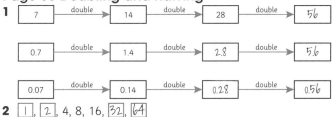

2 1, 2, 4, 8, 16, 32, 64

3 1680
16800
740
7400

4 (a) $6
(b) 8 beads

Page 38 Mental methods for addition and subtraction
1
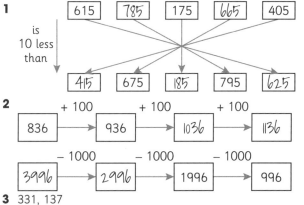

3 331, 137
6, 2083

Page 40 Collecting and representing data
1 12

2

Session	Tally	Total
1	⌿⌿⌿⌿ ⌿⌿⌿	8
2	⌿⌿⌿⌿ ⌿⌿	7
3	⌿⌿⌿⌿ ⌿⌿⌿⌿	9
4	⌿⌿⌿⌿ ⌿	6

3
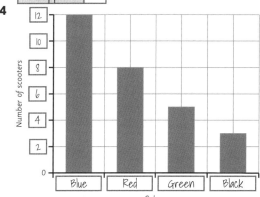

Mango	60
Peach	30
Pineapple	10

4
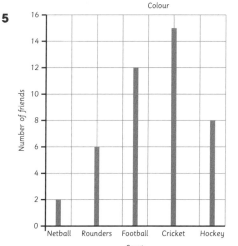

5

Page 42 Interpreting data
1 21

2 (a) 50
(b) 5

3 (a) 5
(b) Yes. 10 chose winter and 5 chose autumn. 5 × 2 = 10
(c) Three times as many students chose summer as chose autumn

4 D

Answers

Page 44 Probability

1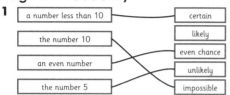

2 **(a)** C

  (b) B

3 **(a)** impossible

  (b)

4 even chance

  even chance

  The answers are the same because there is an equal number of odd and even numbers

5 12

6 Numbers can be placed in any position.

Page 46 Line graphs

1 3°C

  10 am

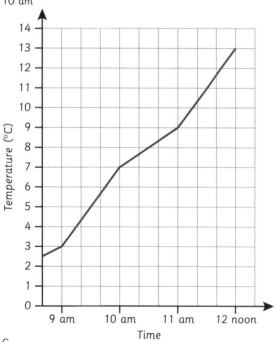

2 C

3 The intermediate points between the dots representing each day do not have any meaning.

Page 48 Finding the mode

1 11°C

2 2

3 47 km

4 4 items

5 He is right. Seven months have 31 days, 4 have 30 days and 1 has 28 days

6 Any combination of numbers that has more 10s than any other number

Page 50 Using scales, drawing and measuring lines

1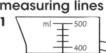

2

3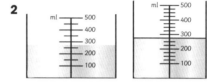

4 45 mm

Page 52 Area and perimeter

2 C and D

3 20 cm

4 perimeter 20 cm

  area 24 cm²

5 perimeter 30 cm

  area 50 cm²

6 **(a)** 42 cm²   **(b)** 36 cm²

  (c) 40 cm²   **(d)** 64 cm²

  (e) 49 cm²   **(f)** 81 cm²

Page 54 Percentages

1 34%, 25%

3 35%, 36%, 72%, 14%, 67%

4 30%, 70%, 90%

5 75%

6 50%, 50%, 75%

7 20%

8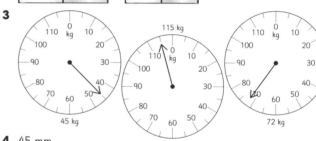

9 60 kg

10 $180

Answers

Page 56 Equivalent fractions, decimals and percentages

1

Fraction	$\frac{1}{10}$	$\frac{2}{10}$	$\frac{3}{10}$	$\frac{4}{10}$	$\frac{5}{10}$	$\frac{6}{10}$	$\frac{7}{10}$	$\frac{8}{10}$	$\frac{9}{10}$	$\frac{10}{10}$	$\frac{1}{2}$	$\frac{1}{4}$	$\frac{3}{4}$
Decimal	0.1	0.2	0.3	0.4	0.5	0.6	0.7	0.8	0.9	1	0.5	0.25	0.75
Percentage	10%	20%	30%	40%	50%	60%	70%	80%	90%	100%	50%	25%	75%

2 $\frac{6}{8}$, $\frac{12}{15}$, $\frac{10}{25}$

4

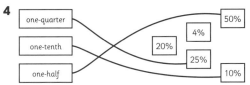

5 $\frac{4}{10}$, $\frac{40}{100}$

6 $\frac{2}{10}$, 0.25, 40%, 0.5

7 $\frac{1}{2}$, 0.55, 0.6, $\frac{65}{100}$

Page 58 Mixed numbers and improper fractions

1 $2\frac{1}{4}$ $2\frac{2}{5}$ $5\frac{1}{3}$ $3\frac{7}{10}$

2 $\frac{1}{4}$ $\frac{1}{2}$ $1\frac{1}{2}$ $1\frac{3}{4}$ 2

3

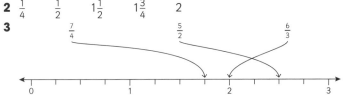

Page 60 Addition and subtraction of decimals

1

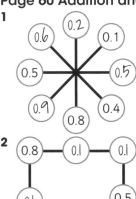

2

0.8	0.1	0.1
0.1		0.5
0.1	0.5	0.4

3 1, 0.7, 0.5

4

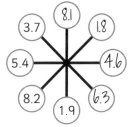

5 10, 2.7, 0.5

6 5.3 + 4.7 or 5.7 + 4.3

7 7.3, 6.5, 4.3, 0.5

Page 62 Division and working with remainders

1 E

2 $6\frac{2}{3}$, $3\frac{1}{5}$

3 **(a)** 28 ÷ 8, 4 packs

(b) 72 ÷ 20, 4 boxes

(c) 4 × 5 = 20, 20 + 1 = 21

(d) 50 ÷ 6, 8 boxes

(e) 18.25 ÷ 2, 10 weeks

4 **(a)** $4

(b) $12

5 **(a)** $4

(b) $8

Page 65 Using inverse operations and brackets

1 $\boxed{62}$ + 38 = 100 $\boxed{32}$ ÷ 4 = 8

83 − $\boxed{55}$ = 28   7 × $\boxed{9}$ = 63

2 50 + 30 = 100 − $\boxed{20}$

150 − 90 = $\boxed{20}$ + 40

4

×	7	5	9
5	35	25	45
4	28	20	36
2	14	10	18

5

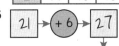

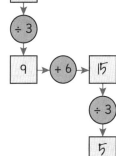

6 9 21

12 11

7 21

7 (14 − 10) + 6 = 10   (20 − 5) − 5 = 10

11 − (6 − 5) = 10   (19 − 14) + 5 = 10

8 20 − ($\boxed{4}$ + 9) = 7   11 − ($\boxed{5}$ − 3) = 9

(9 + $\boxed{2}$) − 3 = 8   (11 − $\boxed{3}$) + 2 = 10

Answers

Page 67 Ratio and proportion

1

	For 4 people	For 8 people
butter beans	650 g	1300 g
stock	350 ml	700 ml
mushrooms	250 g	500 g
tomatoes	400 g	800 g
pumpkin	850 g	1700 g

2

	For 5 children	For 20 children
flour	600 g	2400 g
sugar	400 g	1600 g
butter	450 g	1800 g
eggs	3	12

3 $\frac{1}{5}$

Page 69 Angles

1 40°, 130° and 70°

2 acute, acute, obtuse, obtuse, acute

4 2, 3

5 160°, 25°, 70°

Page 71 Symmetry

1

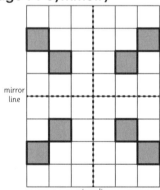

4

	equilateral triangle	square	regular pentagon	regular hexagon
number of lines of symmetry	3	4	5	6
order of rotaional symmetry	3	4	5	6

Page 73 Coordinates and transformations

1 A is (2, 6), B is (1, 5) and C is (4, 2)
4th vertex is (5, 3)

2

 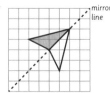

3 The number of sides is the same as the number of lines of symmetry.
The number of sides is the same as the order of rotational symmetry.

4

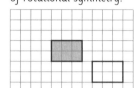

5 3 squares to the left and 1 square up

Page 75 Length, mass and capacity

2
☑ Zina's pencil is 15 cm long
☐ Heidi is 15 m tall
☑ Petra's younger sister weighs 15 kg
☐ Fatima's water bottle holds 15 l

3

	Mass in grams	Mass in kilograms
A watermelon	2000	2
Bag of apples	1400	1.4
Bag of cherries	500	0.5

4 60 cm

5 30 cm

6 fill the jug 4 times (4 × 500 = 2000)

7 5 cm, 55 mm, 55 cm, 5 m

8 200 g, 0.25 kg, $\frac{1}{2}$ kg, 2 kg

9 100mm, 10 cm

10 2 m, 1 litre, 2 kg

Page 78 Using timetables and calendars

1 **(a)** 45 minutes
(b) 1:30
(c) 1 hour 30 minutes

2 **(a)** 46 minutes
(b) 14:46. 16:16

3 19 December

4 5

5 Saturday